Identity: A Very Short Introduction

VERY SHORT INTRODUCTIONS are for anyone wanting a stimulating and accessible way into a new subject. They are written by experts, and have been translated into more than 45 different languages.

The series began in 1995, and now covers a wide variety of topics in every discipline. The VSI library currently contains over 550 volumes—a Very Short Introduction to everything from Psychology and Philosophy of Science to American History and Relativity—and continues to grow in every subject area.

Very Short Introductions available now:

ABOLITIONISM Richard S. Newman
ACCOUNTING Christopher Nobes
ADAM SMITH Christopher J. Berry
ADOLESCENCE Peter K. Smith
ADVERTISING Winston Fletcher
AFRICAN AMERICAN RELIGION
  Eddie S. Glaude Jr
AFRICAN HISTORY John Parker and
  Richard Rathbone
AFRICAN POLITICS Ian Taylor
AFRICAN RELIGIONS
  Jacob K. Olupona
AGEING Nancy A. Pachana
AGNOSTICISM Robin Le Poidevin
AGRICULTURE Paul Brassley and
  Richard Soffe
ALEXANDER THE GREAT
  Hugh Bowden
ALGEBRA Peter M. Higgins
AMERICAN CULTURAL
  HISTORY Eric Avila
AMERICAN HISTORY Paul S. Boyer
AMERICAN IMMIGRATION
  David A. Gerber
AMERICAN LEGAL HISTORY
  G. Edward White
AMERICAN NAVAL HISTORY
  Craig L. Symonds
AMERICAN POLITICAL HISTORY
  Donald Critchlow
AMERICAN POLITICAL PARTIES
  AND ELECTIONS L. Sandy Maisel
AMERICAN POLITICS
  Richard M. Valelly

THE AMERICAN PRESIDENCY
  Charles O. Jones
THE AMERICAN REVOLUTION
  Robert J. Allison
AMERICAN SLAVERY
  Heather Andrea Williams
THE AMERICAN WEST Stephen Aron
AMERICAN WOMEN'S HISTORY
  Susan Ware
ANAESTHESIA Aidan O'Donnell
ANALYTIC PHILOSOPHY
  Michael Beaney
ANARCHISM Colin Ward
ANCIENT ASSYRIA Karen Radner
ANCIENT EGYPT Ian Shaw
ANCIENT EGYPTIAN ART AND
  ARCHITECTURE Christina Riggs
ANCIENT GREECE Paul Cartledge
THE ANCIENT NEAR EAST
  Amanda H. Podany
ANCIENT PHILOSOPHY Julia Annas
ANCIENT WARFARE
  Harry Sidebottom
ANGELS David Albert Jones
ANGLICANISM Mark Chapman
THE ANGLO-SAXON AGE
  John Blair
ANIMAL BEHAVIOUR
  Tristram D. Wyatt
THE ANIMAL KINGDOM
  Peter Holland
ANIMAL RIGHTS David DeGrazia
THE ANTARCTIC Klaus Dodds
ANTHROPOCENE Erle C. Ellis

For more information visit our website

www.oup.com/vsi/

Florian Coulmas

IDENTITY

A Very Short Introduction

OXFORD
UNIVERSITY PRESS

OXFORD
UNIVERSITY PRESS

Great Clarendon Street, Oxford, OX2 6DP,
United Kingdom

Oxford University Press is a department of the University of Oxford.
It furthers the University's objective of excellence in research, scholarship,
and education by publishing worldwide. Oxford is a registered trade mark of
Oxford University Press in the UK and in certain other countries

© Florian Coulmas 2019

The moral rights of the author have been asserted

First edition published in 2019

Impression: 5

Published in the United States of America by Oxford University Press
198 Madison Avenue, New York, NY 10016, United States of America

British Library Cataloguing in Publication Data
Data available

Library of Congress Control Number: 2018958747

ISBN 978-0-19-882854-9

Printed and bound by CPI Group (UK) Ltd, Croydon, CR0 4YY

Contents

Identity

List of illustrations

Identity

Introduction: an 'identity' wave

An obsession is gripping the world—the obsession with identity. In 2015, the Australian National Dictionary Centre selected 'identity' as the Word of the Year. The word is, of course, much older; what the Australians recognized is that it has continued to gain currency for decades. In the 1950s, 'identity' spread around the world, arguably as a by-product of the cultural Americanization then in progress. Today, 'identity' is a household word.

The identity of—the attacker, England, NATO, God's people, neo-tribes, our nation, the group, your cells, plant glutamate receptors, the suspicious substance, statistics, indiscernibles, an endpoint, Kaliningrad, our beloved language, pan-Arabic culture, Leonardo da Vinci's mother, Mr Hyde, legal systems, the Socialist Party, roots, the town centre, the landscape, Ukrainian citizens, twins, women in art, Zhiqing, Jesus Christ, a survivor, Molière, Western civilization—and on and on.

The list of things that are said to have an identity can be extended almost at will. And it can be supplemented by a list of predicates that tell you what kind of identity is at issue: additive, basic, collective, dissociative, cultural, fictitious, linguistic, multiplicative, neuronal, moral, online, political, gender role, stylistic, social, racial, professional, territorial, generational, inherited, genetic,

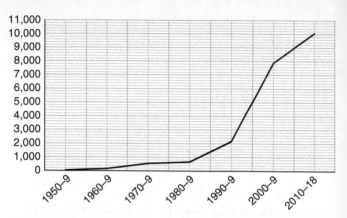

1. Number of English-language books with 'identity' in the title, catalogued in the Library of Congress.

lost, stolen, assumed, fractured, stigmatized, legal, mistaken, true—and on and on.

Talk about identity has become ubiquitous. The number of newly published English-language books that have 'identity' in the title reflects this. The 1950s saw the publication of thirty-seven such books; in the current decade, since 2010, more than 10,000 have appeared (Figure 1).

Sameness and difference, this is what identity is all about. It should be simple, but it isn't. For 'identity' means different things to different people and in different scientific disciplines. Identities are both things that must be explained and things that are invoked to explain. Its protean character allows the notion to adjust with ease to psychological, social, political, cultural, and many other contexts. Some people use it to refer to their personal values, others to designate attachments to ethnic groups, religious communities, or nations. Literary critics' associations with identity differ from those of law enforcement officers. Premordialists believe identity to be fixed, constructivists see it as a work in progress, and interactionists fuse elements of both.

2

Contributing to the identity wave that has engulfed us is the inflation of 'identity crises'. Goldman Sachs suffers an identity crisis, at least according to the *Financial Times*. No need to feel too sorry for him, for Goldman is not a nervous wreck who should be referred to a shrink, but one of the largest banks in the world. The term was once reserved for teenagers stumbling over their own toes, but nowadays anything and everything can be attributed an identity crisis. If someone/something has an identity, then, presumably, they can also have an identity crisis.

Is there anything that has no identity? If we limit our survey to the English-speaking world, the answer is probably 'no'; but if we shift the focus of our attention a little, it appears that in other parts of the world identity is not equally topical. For instance, the Chinese word *shēnfèn* ('identity') refers to the social or legal status of a person, not to larger social units. In postcolonial contexts, discussions about identity have a paradoxical flavour when, in the name of identity, imposed ethnic identities are rejected, as a remnant of the Western domination of the world.

Identity, like all social science categories, is a Western product. This is not to say that it is just a fad, but the ubiquity of identity in Western societies is indicative of its historical contingency as a concept that appeared at a certain time in a certain cultural environment. The intellectual significance of the term 'identity' has not always been as weighty as it is at present. As the concept is understood nowadays, it is first of all rooted in the ideology of the French and American revolutions that celebrated the dignity and equality of the individual. Principles such as one man, one vote, equality before the law, and human rights hinge on the autonomous individual with his or her personal identity. From this individualistic origin, the notion of identity was transferred to collectivities delimited by various shared features, both predetermined and adopted, that claimed a selfhood worth sustaining. In this way, a contradiction emerged that is inherent in the egalitarian democratic idea, that is, obvious inequality in the face of postulated equality.

The topicality of identity is, among other things, a response to this unresolved contradiction, and the preoccupation with it of scholars in diverse fields is part of a general trend in Western societies that goes beyond the confines of academia. The identity wave comes from many sources. It has inspired new insights, but, as we will see, it is also dangerous and carries many substances that pollute the environment.

Core meaning

These preliminary observations suggest that surely the question 'What exactly is identity?' does not have a single answer. This stems from the fact that the word 'identity' is both a technical term of various scientific disciplines and a catchword promiscuously used in ordinary discourse. Words for 'identity' in other European languages are similarly adaptable. In fact, with some odd exceptions (Polish for example), European languages, from French *identité* to Russian *identichnost*, from Dutch *identiteit* to Estonian *identiteet*, share in common the Latin-derived word. Its wide dispersion must be attributed to the self-declared language of Enlightenment, French. This says nothing about the word's present meaning, but it reminds us of its ideological halo.

In medieval Latin whence it was adopted into French, *identitas* means 'the same, sameness, one'. In its entry for 'identity', the second edition of the *Oxford English Dictionary* (OED) still refers to the explanation given in Charles du Cange's 1844 Latin dictionary: 'any repetitive action', which, however, no longer appears in more recent online updates. The OED still highlights 'sameness of a person or thing at all times or in all circumstances' as the principal meaning of the word. If anything should forever stay the same, you might be tempted to think, it is identity. Alas, as the world changes, so does language. For instance, the OED's 2005 update lists 'identity theft', and future updates will reflect further additions and subtle metamorphoses. Dictionaries, therefore, can provide no more than some orientation.

Another approach to identifying the meaning of 'identity' is to examine the words that can be substituted for it in various contexts, for instance, 'authenticity', 'character', 'commonality', 'distinctiveness', 'exclusivity', 'individuality', 'integrity', 'nature', 'quality', 'subject', and 'self'. However, this *Very Short Introduction* is not about words, but about why identity is important in so many different fields.

Many who use the term 'identity' do not care to make their intended meaning explicit. Yet it would not be difficult to parade a couple of dozen definitions of 'identity' here. I only refrain from this exercise because such a list would inevitably invite reproach for ignoring other definitions that undoubtedly exist. Instead, I trust that at the end of each chapter of this book it will be a little clearer than at its beginning what 'identity' means in the chapter's title.

Chapter 1
'Who am I?' Identity in philosophy

Know thyself!

Surely there are things more interesting to ponder than oneself?
Not so fast! Philosophers don't think there are, and they have a point.

As I gaze from my desk across the wide river, I see a flock of
gulls circling around high in the sky. We can describe with great
scientific precision the intricate process it takes for the light waves
to touch my retina and from there to be translated into electrical
impulses that travel through nerve fibres to the occipital lobe of
my brain, where they form an image of a flock of gulls. But where
is the 'I' that sees, and enjoys seeing, the gulls; that decides to look
out of the window rather than answer my email and apply myself
to other chores? Who's in control?

'Know thyself!' Socrates instructed his disciples. For, as he clearly
saw, self-directed thought (*autognosis*) raises the problem that
we must know what knowledge is and who does the knowing.
This became a point of departure for one of the richest fields of
philosophical investigation, from the Socratics through the
'confessions' of Christian thinkers in the medieval period to idealism
and materialism in the modern era.

'Who am I?' is not just about me, but the question guiding the
inquiry into what it is to be human. French writer Michel de

Montaigne (1533–92) echoed Socrates' reasoning two millennia later when he posited, 'every man bears within himself the entire form of the human condition'.

Many Western thinkers followed his lead. Rationalist philosopher René Descartes (1596–1650) explained that I am I because I think (*cogito ergo sum*, in Latin, the language in which he wrote). Being endowed with reason was for him what allows me to say that I exist. John Locke (1632–1704) changed the focus slightly. In addition to rationality, he emphasized a specific kind of self-knowledge, personal memory, as a necessary condition of individual identity. Gottfried Wilhelm Leibniz (1646–1716) thought that the world consisted of infinitely many substances, each located at a point in space, some of which—human minds—were gifted with reason. Because all of these substances, which Leibniz called 'monads', were strictly distinct, everything could be identical just with itself. Georg W. F. Hegel (1770–1831) continued the rationalist tradition of accentuating consciousness as the basis of the individual self. And a century later, Ernst Cassirer still called *autognosis* the supreme purpose of philosophical inquiry.

The question of how consciousness and self-awareness connect with personal identity has accompanied philosophy since antiquity. Sages of diverse orientations have put forth various elaborate answers, showing among other things that self-awareness is more than just being conscious. Yet, it seems a self-sustaining pursuit, producing new puzzles with every solution. That individual identity means being a rational creature with a personal memory is not the end of the story.

I forgot

I still can't remember, but I know there was something I meant to say. Who forgot, and who knows that there was something? Is that the same I or two parts of myself? What was her name again? It begins with an L and has three syllables. No, it wasn't Lolita. Wait, it'll come back to me—but where from? Is my true self the one who forgot or the one who is looking for the three-syllable name, confident of retrieving it; and if so, where does he look if not inside me?

Two related problems arise here: the first concerns identity through time, the second the mind–body problem.

The metaphysics of change already occupied Presocratic thinkers. Parmenides (515–445 BCE) taught, 'there is nothing new under the sun'. The eternal laws of logic make it impossible for something to both exist and not exist, which compels us to admit that real change is impossible. Parmenides' doctrine led to materialism, a worldview that wants to explain everything as movements, collisions, and reconfigurations of unchanging atoms, including the atoms that constitute our sense perceptions and mental events, e.g. admiring gulls in the sky, remembering, and forgetting. In a world like this, the answer to the question, 'who am I?' is this: a collection of physical events, some of which we call mental states and sensations.

Heraclitus' (535 BCE–475 BCE) dictum, 'you cannot step into the same river twice', represents a conflicting position. Everything always changes. This doctrine is compatible with the theory that space-time is constantly fluctuating and the universe expanding. Expansion means real change, and if such is possible, not everything is predetermined and can be reduced to atoms. Evolution may have brought minds into existence, somewhere along the way between the big bang and now. In a world like this, the question 'Who am I?' allows for a dualistic answer making a division of mind and body.

To date, huge progress in science notwithstanding, the case of Parmenides vs Heraclitus isn't settled. We are still stuck with the conundrum of how something/someone can be the same and different, the problem of identity through time.

Essentialism and the Ise Grand Shrine

The Ise Grand Shrine in Mie Prefecture, Japan is the sacred centre of Japan's native Shinto religion. Founded in the 4th century CE, the main shrine buildings have been rebuilt many times. The periodic reconstruction is part of the cult. More than six million pilgrims and tourists come to the shrine every year, and it would not occur to them that they are visiting a replica, though not a single pillar or rafter remains of the 'original' building. Renewal is part of the shrine's spirit, its identity.

Cells in the human body have a limited lifespan and are replaced with new ones all the time. Could we think of ourselves, then, as a kind of walking Ise Grand Shrine? This would be difficult, if only because the shrine is not just renovated regularly, but built up from scratch every twenty years alternatingly on adjacent plots of land. A clone of itself, as it were.

Our identity through time certainly requires as one of its conditions one body rather than two. My clone is not me. However, the notion of our persistence in spite of physical change poses difficulties. One solution is essentialism, a doctrine that once again originates in classical Greek philosophy. To Aristotle, the essence of human beings was rationality, much like the essence of the Grand Shrine is an ideal form associated with certain ideas, rather than material constancy. Descartes harked back to antiquity, taking the position that our identity rests in an immutable essence, the soul. 'Whereas the human body can easily perish', he thought to have proven, 'the soul is immortal by its very nature'. To him the soul is an unextended substance that retains its identity over time.

But where is it? The essence of the Grand Shrine survives periodic dismantlement, but it does not exist without an embodiment. Scientific advancement since the Enlightenment has motivated many philosophers to accept that this is also true for us humans. The most radical and at the same time most consistent view in defiance of Cartesian dualism posits the identity of brain and mind. Which, however, brings us to an important difference between us and the Grand Shrine. Unlike its attic, ours is not rebuilt every twenty years. The regeneration of human brain cells, regrettably, is severely limited. Neurophysiologists consider this the main reason why we become more forgetful with advancing age.

If memory is like a slowly corroding microchip, Locke's idea that memory constitutes self-identity comes under pressure. When we forget irreversibly, we change. This is undeniably what many people experience. Are they still themselves? Many would reject the idea that just because she forgot a name she is no longer herself. After all, she is still her students' professor, her children's mother, her friends' friend, etc. Actually, this is a feature we share with the Grand Shrine. It is what it is by virtue of what people make of it and attribute to it. It is the home of the Sun Goddess and situated in a cedar wood animated by any number of spirits. Our personal identity, too, is to a considerable degree moulded by the people we interact with, who tell us what we are or should be, whom we admire or despise.

Recognizing the social (nurture) influence on individual identity of course does not imply a rejection of biology (nature) as a determinant. Personal identity is not just a convention, something agreed upon by others. Nor do social theories of identity offer an easy way out. There is this photograph of a boy on horseback. That's me, though I haven't gone horseback riding for decades. I'm not *essentially* an equestrian, and I don't look much like the boy on the horse. Still it's me.

Thus we need criteria that enable us to say that a particular person, x_1, at one point in time, t_1, is the same person as x_2 at another point in time, t_2.

Four approaches

Current philosophical approaches that try to provide such criteria are of four kinds: empiricist reductionism, mentalist essentialism, ordinary language analysis, and interactionism.

Reductionism strives to reduce all facts about personal identity to empirically researchable facts about bodies, brains, sense perceptions, behavioural patterns, and how these are interrelated. Personal identity is somatic, consisting of physical matter. A person's enjoyment of watching the gulls in the sky will eventually be explainable in terms of moving particles. Puzzle: what is a person?

Mentalist essentialism is the view that minds (souls) are different from bodies; more than that, they are the essence of people's individual identity. A variety of this view espoused by religious philosophers and theologians holds that a soul can continue to exist after its body dies (e.g. transmigration of souls in Hinduism). Non-religious philosophers can only keep looking for mental processes that establish psychological continuity from t_1 to t_2. Religious thinkers accept the mystery of the soul's God-given nature, as paradigmatically does the dogma of the Catholic Church. Puzzle: when and how is a body ensouled?

Ordinary language analysts take an altogether different approach. Since language is a universal faculty of humanity and since every known language has terms of self-reference, they argue, the logical reconstruction of sentences in which words such as 'I' occur will help us understand what self and hence personal identity is. The sentence 'I enjoy watching the gulls' is fine, while 'My body enjoys watching the gulls' is odd. Why? Puzzle: do children lack an identity before they know how to use 'I' correctly?

Interactionism recognizes the existence of mind and body as two distinct but interacting dimensions of the self, and seeks to overcome the rigid mind–body dualism that has characterized much of Western philosophy for centuries. Rather than accepting an unbridgeable gap between corporeal continuity and psychological continuity, interactionists posit a self-conscious mind able to act on its brain. In this view, trying to recapture the three-syllable name with initial L becomes an activity of the self-conscious mind that deliberately controls neuronal events. Puzzle: with dreams we don't remember, does the brain side-step the self-conscious mind's control when we sleep?

Death and other harms: when is a human being?

At some point, each of the four approaches encounters puzzles, and not just the ones I mentioned. They illustrate that the question regarding the basis on which we should claim identity for ourselves and ascribe it to others is one of the most vexing problems of philosophy. And we have not even touched upon death, Alzheimer's, brain lesions that cause personality changes, the consciousness (or lack thereof) of patients in a persistent vegetative state, schizophrenia, abortion, euthanasia, gene therapy, organ transplantation, and other events that affect our identity, more or less drastically. Awareness of our inevitable passing is a defining characteristic of the human condition, but the beginning and the end of life are associated with unresolved questions of both science and ethics.

Zygotes cannot be self-aware. Are they nevertheless persons with an identity? If so, could life insurance be issued for them? What are the implications of attributing personhood to individual zygotes and embryos for population statistics? Should we make a distinction between persons that can be counted and persons that, perhaps, could be counted in principle but not in fact?

Since, we assume, the zygote has no self-awareness or indeed a psyche, there cannot be psychological continuity between me and the zygote I once was. Since cells both change and are replaced regularly, there is no physical continuity either. In order to determine individual identity, we need an individual. Given the lack of psychological and physiological continuity, it is better to conceptualize the individual as an open system rather than a thing/organism with an essence and clearly delineated boundaries. This will make it easier to adjust our concept of individual identity to our present state of knowledge, although common sense finds it difficult to dispense with fixed categories. 'Identity' above all suggests something given, constant, and immutable; but that is a habit it may be time to rethink.

Autognosis isn't what it used to be

To Socrates, 'know thyself!' meant self-reflection. That hasn't changed; however, the available knowledge about ourselves has changed a great deal. For one thing, in addition to introspection we can know many things about ourselves from sources outside ourselves. Two examples are DNA sequencing for establishing paternity and more distant genealogical relationships, and as a technique to learn about genetic predispositions to disease. Many would find this kind of external knowledge about themselves highly relevant to their identity—the unrecognized heir to a great estate, the racist with reviled blood in his veins.

If we think of individuals as open systems that evolve rather than fixed organisms, we still have to determine in a non-arbitrary way how much and what kind of change individuals can survive and stay the same. A gold filling? No problem. A pacemaker? Hardly worth mentioning. An exchange of blood plus a bone marrow transplant that changes the DNA? A new heart? A tailor-made bionic body? Well, heart to heart, Socrates never had to worry about these questions.

Externalities of this sort are becoming ever less external, giving rise to the question whether my identity is something that 'I' *am*—a dyslexic agnostic insomniac who worries all night about the existence of dog—or something that 'I' *have*: my wedding ring, the dragon tattoo on my bicep, my daily antidepressant?

Anthropo-technology isn't science fiction. It alerts us to the fact that not only individual identity changes and survives change across time, but species identity, too. Manipulable genome-maps, brainpower-enhancement drugs, all-regulating information systems, etc. blur the nature–nurture distinction and that between subject and object of technological intervention, forcing the old question 'Who am I?' to be posed anew (Figure 2).

All the things we do with ourselves nowadays make us see that the individual as a separate coherent self that somehow has to be carried intact from t_1 to t_2 is a creature of Western modernism grown on the fertile ground of European philosophy. The postmodern self is different in that it constructs itself, at least in part, and recognizes this fact. It is inherently fluid, constantly reinventing itself. In this, it is akin to Eastern concepts of personal identity. To mention but one rich tradition, in contrast to European dualism, the holistic view of humanity that Confucianism represents treats the self as an ethical concept predicated on a ceaseless process of self-cultivation and moral improvement.

Conclusions

The question 'Who am I?' has been the starting point of the inquiry into human identity since the earliest days of recorded philosophy and continues to be a principal philosophical concern today. The ensouled matter of the self-conscious brain still poses deeply puzzling questions about individual identity, and nowadays the new reality of anthropo-technology once again poses the question how we can know about ourselves.

2. Socrates' question 'Who am I?' in our time.

Chapter 2
Identity in logic and the classical law of thought

Indiscernibles

In his book *Word and Object* (§24), Willard Van Orman Quine, an influential philosopher of the 20th century, remarked that although the notion of identity is so simple, confusion over it is quite common. The confusion begins with the equals sign '=', which is the most common symbol used in basic arithmetic and logic to express identity:

(1) $x_1 = x_2$, which means
x_1 is the same thing as x_2.

Elementary school pupils are from first grade familiarized with this symbol, which thus becomes such a basic tool of mental operations that most people do not give much thought to it. Until their first class in Logic 101. Logicians do not use terms and symbols lightly, for they are after universal principles and rules of thought. Accordingly, they have produced a huge literature about *identity* and *identification* contemplating the questions of how '=' should properly be used and what it means when it is used properly.

The simplest case is:

(2) Aristotle = Aristotle,

a proposition that asserts that something equals itself. Surely, this is true. According to one influential interpretation, this should be the only logical meaning of *identity*. It is known as *Leibniz's Law* in reference to logician and mathematician Gottfried Wilhelm Leibniz, who argued that any two expressions conjoined by '=' should be interchangeable in all contexts without altering the truth-value of the statements in which they occur (*salva veritate*). While a universal truth, Leibniz conceived of it also as an empirical law that holds for everything. He asserted: 'It is never true that two substances are entirely alike, differing only in being two rather than one.'

Leibniz's reasoning is often illustrated with a story that took place in the garden of Princess Sophie at Herrenhausen (Figure 3). The princess wondered whether in the abundant foliage two identical leaves could be found, which Leibniz denied. He argued that each leaf had features, however minute, that set it apart from all others, a unique identity.

For Leibniz, 'identical' thus meant unique. This interpretation of 'identity' is known as the 'identity of indiscernibles' or the 'indiscernibility of identicals'. Identical objects must have all of their properties in common, including spatial relations with their location and other objects; for otherwise, congruent geometric figures would be counterexamples.

While the identity of indiscernibles could be viewed as a principle to be tested by the instruments and methods of physics and other natural sciences, Leibniz also used the term 'identical' in the sense of identity of meaning, without always making the difference explicit. He distinguished between contingent propositions and identical proposition. The truth of the former depends on the existence of things, whereas the latter are based on the principle of contradiction. Any sentence of the form $x = x$ is an identical proposition, and any sentence of the form $x \neq x$ is a contradiction, regardless of any empirical examination.

3. Leibniz converses with Sophie Charlotte in the park of
Herrenhausen about the possibility of finding two identical leaves.

Taken as a metaphysical principle, the identity of indiscernibles has far-reaching consequences. Most importantly, it is an argument against atomism, more precisely, against atoms as they were comprehended in Leibniz's time, i.e. the smallest hard immutable elements of matter. Without going into the many critical assessments of Leibniz's ideas, suffice it here to point out that the logic of identity is deeply interconnected with our understanding of the natural world.

Because it is rigid and narrow, the notion of 'identity of indiscernibles' is quite clear and logically consistent. However, there are many other ways of asserting identity. A question that arises is whether identity is a relation between objects or between signs (predicates, proper names) and objects. Consider the principle of intersubstitutivity. If x_1 is identical with x_2 then x_1 can be substituted by x_2 in all possible worlds.

For example, let x_1 be 'Aristotle' and x_2 'the son of Nicomachus':

(3)   Aristotle is the son of Nicomachus.

Since Aristotle was indeed the son of Nicomachus, whatever is true of Aristotle should also be true of the son of Nicomachus. The difference between (2) and (3) is that (2) tells you nothing, while (3) tells you something about the world which you may or may not have known. (2) is an analytic sentence, true by virtue of its form, whereas (3) is a synthetic sentence, contingent on the correctness of the information it conveys.

Signs and objects

In everyday discourse, we use sentences of this synthetic form all the time, connecting two expressions with 'is'. The identity relation thus asserted has three properties. It is reflexive, symmetric, and transitive.

Reflexive: a = a

(2) Aristotle is Aristotle (identical with himself).

Symmetric: a = b → b = a

(4) If Aristotle is the son of Nicomachus, then the son of Nicomachus is Aristotle.

For transitivity we need another predicate, for instance, 'a student of Plato's academy', and arrive at the following.

Transitive: a = b and b = c → a = c

(5) If Aristotle is Nicomachus' son, and Nicomachus' son is a student of Plato's academy, then Aristotle is a student of Plato's academy.

It is well known that Aristotle joined Plato's academy, but only when he was 16 or 17 years old. Is (5) therefore false? If so, the substitution test would be imperfect.

This raises the question of 'sense and reference', the title of a famous treatise by logician Gottlob Frege (1848–1925), *Über Sinn und Bedeutung*, which deals with the problem of identity of meaning as it comes to bear when considering sentences such as (2), (4), and (5). If a and b are objects—Aristotle and Nicomachus' son, respectively—it is unsatisfactory (paradoxical) that a is sometimes identical with b, and sometimes not. Frege argues that, therefore, an identity statement 'a = b' must be conceived as a relation holding between signs rather than objects:

> Nobody can be forbidden to use any arbitrarily producible event or object as a sign for something. In that case the sentence a = b would no longer refer to the subject matter, but only to its mode of designation.

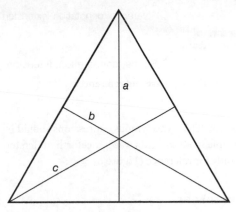

4. Equilateral triangle with three medians.

To deal with the evident difference in the cognitive value of sentence pairs such as 'a = a' and 'a = b' where a and b are designations of the same object, Frege proposes a distinction between the sense (*Sinn*) of a term and its reference (*Bedeutung*). He illustrates this distinction with an equilateral triangle and the intersection point of its medians, *a*, *b*, and *c* (Figure 4). This point can be described as the point of the intersection of *a* and *b*, of *b* and *c*, of *a* and *c*, or of *a*, *b*, and *c*. These descriptions have different senses, but the same reference.

In any universe of discourse, there are, moreover, expressions that have a sense but no reference. Anyone can think up examples, such as, 'the longest English sentence', 'the bachelor's wife', or 'a spacecraft travelling at three times the speed of light'.

Logicians and philosophers in the Aristotelian traditions accepted Frege's tenet, which links identity with the theory of the meaning of signs. To avoid confusion, the reference, or extensional meaning, of an expression must be distinguished from its sense, or intensional meaning. One important consequence of this line of thought was a reinterpretation

Meaning of an expression
- Reference, denotation, extension
- Sense, connotation, intension

5. Two kinds of identity, sense and reference.

of Leibniz's Law. That synonymous expressions should be interchangeable in all contexts was henceforth understood as holding only for reference (Figure 5).

Types and tokens

In ordinary language, sense and reference are not always held apart, which sometimes results in ambiguity. For instance, one could say that (6) contains ten words or five words:

(6)   'T is so much joy! 'T is so much joy!

Both are true; however, in this stanza from Emily Dickinson's poem, we are counting different things, ten words, but five *different* words, distinguished, respectively, as 'tokens' and 'types'. But what are types? Some philosophers say they are universals with no spatio-temporal existence. Others say they are abstract objects of the mind, and still others conceive of types as sets comprising all actual and possible tokens of them. Think of the letters of the Latin alphabet. Each of them is an abstraction, a mental image defining a set of all possible letters that are recognized as A, B, C, etc. Clearly, then, a token is only a token relative to a type. Conversely, a type exists only through its tokens. In this interpretation, it is impossible to have a type without at least one token.

The type–token relationship has implications for the concept of identity in many different fields, such as identical words, identical notes, identical sensations, identical photographs, identical calendar years, and identical aeroplanes. It has been widely discussed and has been linked to the mind–body problem. In all cases, to avoid confusion and logical paradox, it is imperative to make a clear distinction between type identity and token identity.

Fuzzy identity

The world of classical logic is a world of the excluded middle. There is no room for 'quite true' and 'mainly false'. The predicates that express identity are discrete and clearly defined. The range of possible kinds of objects for which a predicate holds—its extension in the sense of Frege's theory of meaning—is determined unequivocally.

In the real world, there are questions. Is this a creek or a river? Is Humpty Dumpty clever? How far away from the summit can you be and still truthfully say you are on Mount Fuji? Because it cannot handle vagueness, classical logic has no answers to these questions. Philosophers have been divided as to whether vagueness is a property of mental representations, of linguistic descriptions, or of things of the world. Russell famously denied that there are vague things, insisting that vagueness is a matter of imprecise representation.

Wittgenstein emphasized the role of language. His notion of how logic and the world are connected still reverberates today. As he saw it, we cannot accept that the world could disobey the laws of logic because 'we could not *say* of an "unlogical" world how it would look'. The general question revolving around 'identity' is this: what does how we speak imply about what there is? Does the fact that there are vague expressions imply that there are vague objects? For our topic, this is a crucial question, for many predicates essentially important to our lives are inherently vague: adult, male, intelligent, dead, alive, healthy, normal, drunk, and on and on.

In response to the limitations of classical logic with regard to vagueness, other logics arose, notably *fuzzy logic*, and in recent years, the ontology of vague objects has become a new field of inquiry explored, for instance, by philosopher Michael Morreau. Velocity is a pertinent example. Classical logic is confined to 'fast' (= 'not slow') and 'slow' (= 'not fast'), while fuzzy logic operates with a variable velocity and three fuzzy sets, 'slow', 'average', and 'fast' with variable membership values. Fuzzy logic has a fuzzy notion of truth and allows for truth-value gaps, that is, propositions that are neither true nor false.

Russell once remarked that 'no one outside a logic-book ever wishes to say "x is x"'. Yet it is hard to part with the principle that things are identical with themselves and harder still to imagine a world where this principle does not imply sharp boundaries of all things for which it holds. However, both biology and physics have moved in the direction of accepting vague material objects and organisms, although this does not mean that the ontology of vague objects is uncontested. Vague objects can be conceived as persisting through time and being identical with themselves only in the non-Leibnizian sense that they have temporal parts. They are comparable to social entities such as cities, political parties, nations, and tribes, which lack sharp boundaries as the relations of membership in these entities is indeterminate. Fuzzy logic attempts to make up for the shortcomings of classical logic, while holding on to a concept of identity which, while admitting vagueness, is still based on the individual.

Non-Western approaches

As the discussion so far has shown, the question of identity in logic cannot easily be separated from the question of a coherent worldview. It is not surprising, therefore, that outside classical logic we find different conceptions of 'identity'. In Buddhist philosophy as developed by Dignāga (480 CE–540 CE) and Dharmakīrti (died 660 CE), for example, identity plays a role as identity of essence and identity of extension, much as in Frege's logic of sense and reference. However, the thinking on which these concepts rest is distinctive.

In the Aristotelian tradition, the individual is the basis of all classification and hence of all thought. The problem of vagueness leads to the somewhat artificial construction of the self-sameness of individuals that persist through time by virtue of having temporal parts. In Buddhist logic, by contrast, the impermanence of all being is the point of departure. Like Western thinkers, Buddhist philosophers grappled with the problem of how cognition, language, and the world are related; however, unlike the former, the latter do not take as given the 'world out there', and they do not proceed from the assumption that its secrets are for us to uncover. Ultimate knowledge of the material world is not possible. A consequence for the notion of 'individual' acknowledged by many Buddhist philosophers is that, rather than being characterized by positive properties, the individual is characterized negatively. The doctrine of non-self (Sanskrit *anātman*) is at the heart of identity (Sanskrit *tādātmya*).

Identity is established by exclusion:

(7) $x = -(-x)$,
x is not not-x.

In Buddhist thought, the inclusion of its own negation is a dialectic relationship, negation being understood as a basic category, rather than the absence of a category. An object is recognized as what it is by a process of excluding everything that is not that object. In this conceptualization of the individual, change is inherent, which also has implications for universals. Some Buddhist thinkers reject universals altogether, and for those who do acknowledge universals, they do not exist as immutable Platonic ideal forms, but only in the mind.

Tādātmya is a non-essentialist concept of identity that rests on the faculty of distinguishing 'from the other'. It has been called 'identity in difference' and is in this sense suggestive of conceptualizations of 'identity' nowadays current in the social sciences. According to the most basic Buddhist principles of reasoning, identity is a construct rather than a state of affairs; it is in the mind, not in the world; for in the ever-changing reality perfect sameness is impossible. The individual is not understood as an isolated entity, but as an interrelated part of the impermanent universe. Nevertheless, there is also permanence, for the universe follows two eternal principles: spirit and substance. The former is stable, the latter fluid. Logic is a matter of spirit conforming to the basic principles of thought, negation, and contradiction, which do not change.

These two principles are understood in like manner in East and West; yet they are applied in the logic of identity differently. This is important to keep in mind, as scholars dealing with identity in other disciplines invariably insist that their thinking obeys the laws of logic.

Conclusions

Leibniz's law of the identity of indiscernibles conforms to the laws of logic. It defines identity as strict self-sameness, which is consistent, but raises the difficult problem of what counts as the same. By framing identity as a semantic problem and introducing a distinction between the meaning of an expression (sense) and what it stands for (reference), Frege provided a partial solution to it, but vagueness continues to pose a major difficulty for the logic of identity. Non-Western logics that differ from the Aristotelian tradition offer an alternative in that they view every concept as including its own negation as a property, rather than the absence of properties.

Chapter 3
Given or constructed?
Identity in cultural
anthropology

'I became a black man when
I arrived in England'

If 'Who am I?' is a tricky question, 'Who are we?' is hardly less troublesome, being grounded as it is in today's identity obsession. Humanity is one, but at the same time divided into multiple groups. Scattered around the globe, humans exhibit many variations in terms of race, language, religion, descent and kinship, residential patterns, use of tools, dress, diet, and so on. These features constitute 'ethnicity', marking what seem to be clear distinctions; yet their usefulness for a coherent classification is limited. They are contingent, and hence subject to perpetual change, and they are vague, allowing for partial and shifting attachment. What is more, how we see ourselves often does not match how others see us.

Writer Inua Ellams made the point succinctly. In autumn 2017, his *Barber Shop Chronicles* was staged in London to considerable acclaim. The play tackles the 'African male', or rather the peculiarly homogeneous idea of the African male in the UK. In a newspaper interview, Ellams remarked, 'I became a black man when I arrived in England'. He *is* a black man, but during his childhood in Nigeria, his blackness was never an issue. It had no important role in the formation of his identity; in England, it became a central part of it.

Ethnographic imagination

Cultural anthropology, a natural child of Western colonialism, has for decades tried to identify ethnicities or ethnic groupings for the purpose of study, soliciting the help of physical anthropology. Under the influence of Charles Darwin's pioneering work on evolution, the 19th century saw a wealth of racial theories about the human species, many of which built on, or degenerated into, unscientific racist doctrines.

The colonialist expansion had led European scholars to discover the 'wisdom of the Indians', the 'Chinese scientific genius', and made them salute *ex oriente lux* ('out of the east, light comes'). However, their appreciation of other 'high' civilizations did little to undermine the general assumption of the white man's superiority, which legitimized the continuation of slavery, domination, and exploitation, in spite of the Enlightenment's ideals of freedom and equality, which were all-inclusive only in name.

The catastrophes of the 20th century, notably the extermination of Jews in the Shoah, discredited the most blatant forms of racism, but racialist notions proved to be hard to eradicate completely from the investigation of humanity's ethnic multitude. It was only in the 1980s, when major progress in genetic research gave rise to the monogenesis theory of a common African ancestry of humanity, that skin colour and other physical traits were recognized as adaptive features of discordant groups rather than distinguishing human races. Ever since, human biologists have mostly discarded race as a meaningful category.

Ethnographers, however, sustained their project of separating groups and subgroups, replacing race by culture, understood as the ensemble of artefacts, customs, beliefs, and institutions accepted by a group. Small groups living in remote areas held the promise of presenting primeval ways of life uncorrupted by modernity and were therefore, for some time, the ethnographers' preferred object of investigation. They were always marginal and are more so today. Already in the 1930s, French cultural anthropologist Claude Lévi-Strauss entitled his study of the secluded Nambikwara in the wilds of Brazil *Tristes Tropiques* (*Sad Tropics*), knowing that their way of life was doomed. Stagnation means death.

Modern civilization has left few areas untouched. As global capitalism spreads, commodities, technologies, and populations circulate around the globe with increasing intensity, pushing many indigenous peoples to the brink of extinction. This does not mean that humanity fuses into one big homogeneity or that a uniform global culture is emerging. But instead of forever hunting for the pristine and primordial in order to unveil the *essence* of a culture, ethnographers have taken also to investigating the fuzzy edges and the seams that hold the colourful tapestry of groups and subgroups together and, at times, come undone.

Ethnicity and cultural identity are not timeless and static, nor do they show any sign of being soaked up by the whirlwind of globalization. Because people want them, they persist. Fredrik Barth and his colleagues pointed the way when, in the 1960s, they gave attention to people who change their ethnic membership, and proposed what is now known as a *constructivist view of identity*. Almost three decades later, the title of a book by Belgian ethnographer Eugeen Roosens captured the essence of this paradigm shift, *Creating Ethnicity*.

Ethnic identity is acquired at birth. The legacy of the group into which they are born is inherited by newborns by fate, forming the only reality they know for some time. Yet changes and various degrees of affiliation are possible. This is why establishing unequivocal and stable boundaries of ethnicities is difficult. Rather than upholding their ancient tradition, many ethnic groups are the result of relatively recent fission or fusion. Criteria

29

of likeness and difference on which ethnic identity is based are selective. They may be foregrounded or suspended, as desired or expedient.

Until the dissolution of the multiethnic Yugoslav state, the population of Bosnia-Herzegovina consisted of Bosnians, Croats, and Serbs. In the course of the war of the early 1990s, Islam, which in Yugoslavia was 'just a religion', became the defining feature of Bosnian ethnic loyalty, producing the 'Muslim Bosniak' ethnicity.

A group's ethnic identity always unfolds in its relationships with other groups, and it depends on the nature of these relationships how permeable its boundaries are. The ethnically homogenous nation state is a rare exception. Hence ethnic groups interact with other ethnic groups at various levels and degrees of intensity within the overarching framework of a state.

Administrative classification

It took time for the constructivist approach to ethnicity to trickle through to the offices of census bureaus and national administrations. This is understandable, for constructivism doesn't mean ethnic identities aren't real. Or race, for that matter. Quite the opposite, administrative classifications have done much to enhance ethnic differences, giving them salience.

Governments highlight or deny ethnic identities, with or without the consent of those concerned. Thus an important aspect of group delimitation to note in this connection is power, which makes us see that, rather than the quasi-natural fruit of evolution, ethnic identities are often the result of conflict. And they lead to conflict in turn. Examples are not far to seek.

In 1994, clashes between the Hutu majority of Rwanda and the Tutsi minority exploded into the genocide of an estimated 800,000 Tutsis (and other minorities). The conflict was the legacy of ethnic boundaries drawn in colonial times. Genetically, Hutu and Tutsi are close relatives of Bantu extraction. Centuries of living together and much intermarriage have blurred the boundaries between them, but once distinguished for whatever administrative purposes by the Belgian colonial government, the division provided a reason for interethnic strife.

At around the same time, in the Bosnian war of 1992–5, which broke out in the wake of the dissolution of Yugoslavia, Serbian troops killed more than 100,000 Muslim Bosniaks. Before the war, Serbs, Croats, and Bosnians had lived together more or less peacefully, but when the Socialist Federal Republic of Yugoslavia broke apart and the pledge of intergroup tolerance with it, ethnic fault lines re-emerged with devastating force. Again, genetic differences between the three groups cannot motivate discrimination; and whatever linguistic differences exist between Serbian, Croatian, and Bosnian hardly hamper communication. Thus, religion served as the principal criterion of demarcating identities.

When faith can be made to dance to the tune of interethnic hatred, piety does not protect against violence, as many other examples testify. Since independence, India has been unable to prevent ordinary Hindus and Muslims from falling into bloody conflict time after time, because, psychoanalyst Sudhir Kakar argues, traditional religious identifications are the most potent formative force in early childhood.

In Myanmar, too, religion bears the main potential for conflict, pitting the Theravada Buddhist majority against the Muslim minority. Since 2015, the Rohingya, who have been living in the western Myanmar province of Rakhine for generations, have fled violence at the hands of the Myanmar military and Buddhist vigilantes by the hundreds of thousands and sought refuge in neighbouring Bangladesh, a Muslim majority country. In the past also known as 'Chittagonians' (under British rule) and 'Muslim

Arkanese', the Myanmar government calls them 'Bengali', thus denying them citizenship and a rightful place on Myanmar state territory.

Ascription and assertion

Religion, language, and race are the most salient criteria of ethnic classification and identity. But they do not exist in a vacuum. An important distinction in any discussion of ethnic identity is between *asserted* and *ascribed* identity, which comes to the fore whenever one does not match the other. The story of Zuvdija Hodžić, born in Gusinje, Montenegro, as told by political scientist Bohdana Dimitrovova, illustrates this:

> I came to Istanbul and people asked me, 'Who are you?' I said, 'a Turk', but they shook their heads: 'Eh, you are not, you are Albanian'. So I came to Skadar as Albanian, where I was told that I was Bosniak. So I went to Sarajevo as Bosniak and people around me asked me again what I was, and I said, 'Bosniak'. They thought I was mad and told me that I was Montenegrin, but with Islamic religion. Then, in Podgorica, someone said to me that I was nothing but a Turk. Who am I, and what am I? Nobody.

As Zuvdija Hodžić found out, you are not necessarily what you think you are. His case highlights three important points. First, he thinks he can associate himself with the ethnic group of his choice; second, the group he wants to associate with may reject his bid; and third, that worries him. Rather than saying 'Who cares?' in the face of rejection, he comes to the disconcerting conclusion that he is nobody.

Most people do not want to be nobody and consider belonging to a community of faith, language, or race a safeguard against such an uninviting fate. Ethnic identities are not fixed, but are to some extent permeable. They include elements of

assertion and ascription, although assertion is not always
successful, and ascription not always refused.

Singapore's ethnic classification provides an example. The British
administration perceived the colony's population as consisting of
a wide variety of 'races' including Cantonese, Hokkiens, Hylams,
Khehs, Straits-born Chinese, Malays, Sumatrans, Javanese,
Buginese, Boyanese, Tamils, Malayalis, Punjabis, Pathans, Sikhs,
Sindhis, Europeans, and Eurasians. After independence, the
Singapore government fused all of these into four groups, Chinese,
Malays, Indians, and Others. Like the evidently arbitrary 'Others',
the remaining three categories were internally heterogeneous,
but over the decades this classification acquired a social reality,
as the Singaporeans gradually accepted it and developed a sense
of (Singaporean) Indianness, Malayness, and Chineseness.

The amalgamation of these three groups has various consequences,
for example, regarding the languages of public services and
instruction at school. It exemplifies the malleability of ethnic
boundaries and at the same time, ironically, underscores the
tendency of socially constructed ethnic identities to assume an
essential quality to their adherents. Singapore has been largely
successful in avoiding community strife by reducing and ordering
difference. Perhaps the administrative classification makes
everyone realize that it involves a measure of arbitrariness, which
works against exaggerated essentialism.

In Singapore, as in Europe much earlier, the principal thrust of
ethnic dynamics was to create larger groups. But this is not a
single march in the direction of higher levels of ethnic integration.
While Singapore created more inclusive categories, China moved
from distinguishing only four groups in addition to the Han
Chinese—Manchus, Mongolians, Tibetans, and Koreans—at the
beginning of the 20th century, to fifty-six officially recognized
ethnic minorities, at the end. Similar developments occurred in

independent India. The constitution of 1950 introduced the term 'Scheduled Tribes', of which the government gradually recognized more than 700. The United States and Western Europe, too, experienced an 'ethnic revival', in which subnational groups were increasingly seen as indispensable building blocks of society.

Appreciation of ethnic diversity is historically contingent. The epoch of decolonization after World War II brought with it recategorizations, both in newly independent states and in Western European countries where continuing in-migration motivated new distinctions. For instance, Malaysia introduced the category Bumiputera (literally 'sons of the land') to distinguish Malays and other indigenous peoples of South East Asia from Chinese and Indian immigrants. Similarly, the Netherlands experimented with distinguishing Autochtonen and Allochtonen, the latter comprising all persons with at least one parent born overseas. However, in 2016 the Dutch government abandoned this classification as unsuitable for separating 'us' from 'them', the native from the foreign.

Census data and immigration regimes provide further examples of changing ethnic classifications. For instance, the 1860 US census had just three race categories: White, Black, and Mulatto. The 1900 census collected data on 'Color or Race' as follows: '"W" for White, "B" for Black, "Ch" for Chinese, "Jp" for Japanese, or "In" for American Indian'. From 1920 until 1940, it counted all persons originating from India as 'Hindus', regardless of religion, language, or skin colour. In 1930, Hispanics were first counted as their own race/ethnic group, but not in subsequent censuses. Since 1980, renewed attempts were made to count Hispanics, which, however, proved difficult and the issue is not settled. Of late, the standards used for official data collection proposed in the US contain five categories for race: American Indian or Alaska Native, Asian, Black or African American, Native Hawaiian or other Pacific Islanders, and White. In 2014, the Census Bureau added MENA as another category, Middle Eastern and North African.

Voluntary attachment and loyalty

Every country's ethnic classification mirrors its history of migration; at the same time, the diversity of national standards is also indicative of the general difficulty of finding universal criteria for categorizing ethnicities. Max Weber, one of the founding fathers of sociology, was aware of this and, therefore, grounded his theory of community formation not in seemingly objective—i.e. biological—criteria such as race and innate ties of ancestry, but in perceived distance and cultivated exclusiveness, which in combination make for group identity. For Weber, an ethnic group was a social rather than a natural fact.

For a long time, this insight remained academic and was of little practical consequence, but finally some governments have recognized self-identification as the proper method of determining a person's ethnicity, in effect relativizing if not eliminating the ascribed/asserted distinction. The British Office of National Statistics declares:

> In ethnic group questions, we are unable to base ethnic identification upon objective, quantifiable information as we would, say, for age or gender. And this means that we should rather ask people which group they see themselves as belonging to.

Similarly, the US Census Bureau nowadays defines race as:

> a person's self-identification with one or more social groups. An individual can report as White, Black or African American, Asian, American Indian and Alaska Native, Native Hawaiian and Other Pacific Islander, or some other race. Survey respondents may report multiple races.

The final point is particularly noteworthy; for until the mid-20th century race classification in the US was 'objective' and binary, rather than fuzzy. People were white or, in accordance with the 'one-drop rule' (if they had even one distant forebear of sub-Saharan ancestry), non-white. What is one to say about the concept of one person belonging to multiple races? Is not the whole point of ethnic/racial classification clear-cut distinction? How much sense does it make to permit multiple affiliations? On one hand, it seems to say, 'do as you please', indicating that race isn't really important; on the other hand, it reconfirms the importance of race by holding on to the category instead of discarding it altogether.

Actually, the apparent contradiction reflects the present state of affairs with regard to racial and ethnic identity in many societies where racial/ethnic discrimination is an everyday occurrence. Lack of objective criteria—biological essences—for ethnic identification does not undercut the importance attached to perceived ethnic identities of one's own group and others.

Stereotypes and ethnocentrism

If we, the Xs, know that the Ys are lazy, unwashed, deceitful, and irresponsible, in short, barbarians, this is very useful; for then we know that we don't want our daughters and sons to marry a Y, sit next to a Y on the underground, or have anything else to do with the Ys. Stereotypes make life easier, relieving us of the need to think. Which is most probably why stereotyping is ubiquitous. It helps us navigate through our busy lives, since we needn't stop to contemplate what to make of every single encounter, fleeting as it may be. In many cases, we already know and can thus direct our attention to other things. As painful experience has taught, stereotyping of other groups that solidifies into ethnic prejudice is found in most ethnic communities, however defined.

The counterpart of stereotyping is ethnocentrism, which is similarly widespread. One's own group is the centre of the universe. Belief systems and worldviews are ethnocentric in that they explain everything from the point of view of one's group and give every event symbolic meaning with reference to it. The idea of the 'chosen people' is an extreme form of ethnocentrism, implying that others, because of whatever deficit they may suffer from, were not chosen. We find ethnocentric attitudes of variable intensity in groups of every size, including highly complex societies, where they may become indistinguishable from nationalism. In Japan, for instance, the belief in physical and cultural homogeneity and uniqueness is widespread, as is a sense of superiority in China.

A challenge to pluralistic societies

Because ethnocentrism implies a claim to the right to follow one's own rules and conventions, it poses a challenge to modern pluralistic societies committed to a democratic ethos of equality. Western societies have learnt that the melting pot ideology does not go down well with many who insist on having their own ethnic identity, no matter where. A geographic habitat once was part of the ethnographer's concept of ethnic identity, even with regard to nomads. Nowadays, heritage cultivation has replaced attachment to one's ancestral homeland, and, accordingly, one can assert one's Sicilian identity in New York, partake in Vietnamese identity in Paris, enjoy Turkish identity in Berlin, and attend the annual Samba festival in Kobe (Figure 6).

Ahmed Aboutaleb was born in Beni Sidel, Morocco. He moved to the Netherlands when he was 15, to be elected Mayor of Rotterdam some three decades later. Since 2016, Sadiq Khan, son of a working-class British Pakistani family, has been the Mayor of London. Born in San Fernando, Spain, Anne Hidalgo became a French citizen at the age of 14. In 2014 she was elected Mayor of Paris. These three rather prominent politicians, among many others, represent the demographic dynamics that have changed Western societies and helped to temper ethnocentrism and stereotyping.

6. Whose ethnic identity? The annual Samba festival in Kobe, organized by Japanese return migrants from Brazil.

Like Aboutaleb, Khan, and Hidalgo, many recent immigrants and citizens with a migration background transcend ethnic boundaries. At the same time, a growing number of people have, and identify themselves as having, mixed ethnic origins. That census bureaus and other administrative agencies allow for multiple self-affiliation is a response to these developments.

Of course, statistics do not solve problems; they can only help us understand the situation. The picture of ethnic multitude today is complex. Modernization has been characterized by the consolidation of nation states and the formation of larger units accompanied by discrimination and assimilation pressure. Continuing migration has concomitantly worked as a countertendency, making many urban environments more ethnically diverse. Yet the conflict potential associated with ethnic intergroup relationships remains, as the more inclusive identity of the big city does not always displace the less inclusive 'heritage' identities of migrants, or their marginalization by the dominant majority. As a response, self-segregation is a noticeable trend among many groups whose

38

members embrace ethnic identities to counterbalance the individualization of urban life and reduce the risk of being nobody.

Conclusions

The increased presence of immigrants in urban centres of the West has raised public awareness of ethnic identity. Cultural anthropologists understand this kind of identity as distinguishing population groups whose members agree on traits that set them apart from others, notably race, language, and religion. While members of groups thus defined tend to think of these criteria as fixed, they are social rather than natural. Therefore, ethnic identities can adjust to changing circumstances, although the members who affiliate with an ethnicity may be convinced of its intransience.

Chapter 4
Adam and Eve, Hijra, LGBTQs, and the shake-up of gender identities

Contingent sins

Boys and girls (in this order), *tertium non datur* (a third is not given). This is the two-valued gender logic of Christianity; or was, until recently. It is no exaggeration to say that for the majority of Christians, the story of Adam and Eve (Genesis 2:4–3:24) was for generations all there was to say about the nature of human sexuality (at least, to be said aloud). Conservative and fundamentalist Christian denominations still insist that heterosexual monogamy is what the Bible prescribes and consider homosexuality a sin. That morals and attitudes about sexuality are historically and culturally contingent they do not want to know or acknowledge, sticking to a worldview epitomized (rather beautifully, though) by Albrecht Dürer's engraving (Figure 7), a natural division into males and females.

To be sure, Christians are not alone in their censure of homosexuality. Islam, like Christianity a creed that has missionary ambitions and universalistic pretensions, has been widely interpreted as proscribing homosexual acts. There are in Islamic as well as in Christian countries various positions and legal regimes concerning sexual behaviour. What they share in common is a general intolerance of non-conformity, treating homosexual practices at various times as immorality, mental illness,

7. **The two-valued logic of gender:** *Adam and Eve* by Albrecht Dürer, 1504.

or criminal offence. The third Mosaic religion, Judaism, likewise traditionally prohibits homosexual conduct.

Turning to other creeds and cultures, the Greek gods of antiquity did not restrict sexual activity morally or legally to reproduction. Portrayals of beautiful young men such as Ganymede whom even gods admired are plentiful on vase paintings, as are erotic stories involving men in Greek literature. And the female poet Sappho of Lesbos gave name to female same-sex orientation (lesbianism).

The Kathoey of Buddhist Thailand, composed of intersex people, is a group that defies binary gender distinction. Many, including many of their own, categorize them as a third sex. Similar attitudes obtained in Theravada Buddhist countries such as Myanmar and Sri Lanka, which had no legal provisions against homosexuality before colonial times. Only the British introduced legal statutes against it. Hinduism also held rather accepting views about same-sex relations, Sanskrit text mentioning men and women who behave like the opposite sex, as determined at the time of their birth. Accordingly, India's complex system of castes, tribes, religious communities, and social groups includes recognized third-gender groups, the Hijra and Aravani (bisexuals, transgender people, and eunuchs) being the most prominent.

Taoism (also *Daoism*), an ancient religious and philosophic tradition of China that emphasizes harmony with 'the way' (*dao*), entertains what must be among the most tolerant attitudes towards variations of sexual relationships. Its Yin Yang symbol of two intertwined swirls—each encompassing, and merging into, the other—is suggestive of the idea that female and male, night and day, passivity and activity imply each other, that there are shades between them, that everything is both constant and cyclical, and that opposites constitute a unity.

These examples are sketchy, ignoring the diversity of views within each faith, but they tell us that sexual morals are variable, and with them gender roles and gender identities. Change in these matters tends to be gradual and often goes unnoticed; however, the past generation has witnessed conspicuous changes, with regard to our knowledge about the biology of human sex determination, about the social formation of gender identities, and about the Western fascination with 'coming out'.

Shift of gender identities

Perhaps the most consequential change in the Western world was the conceptual separation of sex and gender. This distinction, with which today most people are familiar, is actually quite new. It did not gain wider currency before the late 1970s. There is some variation in how the terms *sex* and *gender* are used, but on the whole, the former is more related to the innate characteristics of genes and hormones, while the latter encompasses learnt characteristics, socio-cultural expectations and patterns of behaviour. The interaction of both has an influence on how individuals see themselves and how they relate to others.

This is nothing new, and as long as in a society the social contract regulating relations between the sexes is generally accepted, there is little reason to question the meaning of femininity and masculinity. These quasi-natural attributes everyone understands. But at times relations between the sexes are out of kilter and therefore become topical. In the Western world, the feminist liberation movement that emerged after World War I and picked up steam after World War II embodied and spearheaded a major shift in the established order.

Initially the movement targeted the oppression of women by men, especially in the labour market, which men had dominated since the industrial revolution. Subsequently its focus shifted to emphasizing and celebrating women's difference. Since women and men are not just women and men, but also citizens, participants in a capitalist economy, members of religious and ethnic groups, etc., feminists advanced various different theories about female identity and gender discrimination. A major division is between two distinct positions:

(1) Women behave like women because they have been oppressed for generations (and therefore should change their behaviour and that of men).

(2) Women behave like women because they are women, being as they are fundamentally different from men (and therefore should fight for recognition of difference).

For our purposes, the question which one of these positions is preferable can be left unanswered. But we should take note of the fact that in the wake of the feminist critique of capitalist society the entire binary order of male and female experiences, identities, values, and norms came under pressure. And what we should ask is why this happened when it did.

Socio-economic determinants of gender identities

The conceptual distinction of sex and gender takes the wind out of the sails of those who are ideologically committed to the discrimination of women as God-given or fixed by nature. Until well into the 20th century, conservative men, but by no means only men, regularly invoked nature to legitimize unequal treatment of women in political and economic life. But as the insight gained ground that natural differences between the sexes are moulded by social gender roles, a fundamental review of the established order became possible. Gender identities were now seen as partly given, partly made.

However, it wasn't just advancement in our knowledge or the success of the Women's Liberation Movement that drove change in the direction of more equality. Gender roles interact with other social conditions. In the Western world, the homemaker–breadwinner division of labour along gender lines was for a long time economically functional, and thus rarely contested. But as coincident with progressing industrialization and the expansion of the service sector the female labour

Labour force participation rate is the proportion of the population aged 15 and older that is economically active. All figures correspond to 'modeled ILO estimates'.

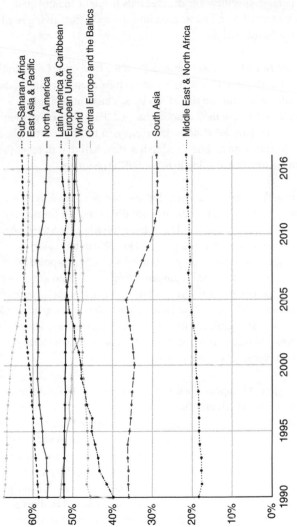

8. **Female labour force participation in early industrial countries over time.**

participation rate increased (Figure 8), the objective measure of gender-specific wage differentials brought the unequal treatment of men and women into the spotlight, giving rise to the feminist critique.

At the same time, most Organisation for Economic Co-operation and Development (OECD) countries have seen a decline of the fertility rate and the size of families. The demographic characteristics of motherhood changed. For instance, women in the UK bore 3.5 children on average in 1900. A century later, the fertility rate had declined to less than half that number (1.64), similar trends occurring in other OECD countries.

It would be naïve to assume that the number of children per family diminished because women didn't like mothering any more, or that they entered the labour force because they longed for 'self-realization' through a paid job. When one salary isn't enough to feed the family, two must work. Socio-political discussions and moral arguments respond to, and at times reinforce, economic changes, which in the event found expression in society-wide contestations of gender roles. Since gender roles are instilled in children from the earliest age, as they learn the values and interactional norms of the society in which they grow up, change does not happen overnight.

But when it happens the question what it is to be feminine or masculine, which may have lain dormant for a long time, resurfaces. Not too long ago, many people would have considered 'female trucker' and 'male nurse' incongruous (and some still do). Engineering, construction, accounting, and law were more or less exclusively male domains, whereas elementary school teachers, secretaries, nurses, and cashiers were overwhelmingly female. As long as both men and women believed in divergent natural talents and aptitudes, this wasn't much of an issue, especially because men and women work in different occupations in countries around the world, which lends credence to the notion of natural dispositions. However, the feminist critique addressed occupational segregation head-on, turning gender into a focal element of the identity discourse.

Theories about occupational segregation focus on different aspects of gender division of labour. Some assume that men and women have different preferences. Because of their family orientation, women attach less importance to their professional life than men do. Others see the discrimination of women in the workplace originating in male workers' dislike of working with women. Given this, every woman hired will disrupt the work process reducing managers' willingness to employ women. Yet other theories have emphasized statistical discrimination in the sense that employers hire staff based on their experience, which tells them that male applicants have higher average skills.

An innovative approach is *identity economics*. Developed by George Akerlof and Rachel Kranton, two US economists, it has brought occupational segregation home to economic theory. In the past, economists have ignored identity, treating it, like tastes and preferences, as individual characteristics. By contrast, identity economics relates personality traits to identities (gender, ethnic, racial). Identity, norms, and social categories together define people's social position and influence their decisions. People see themselves as belonging to social categories—a mother at home, a professional at work, a foreigner at a Parent Teacher Association meeting—and adjust their behaviour to the norms pertaining to them.

Identity economics reckons with identities and the norms associated with them as factors of (economic) decision making, i.e. calculating individual gains and losses from different decisions. It can help to explain the fact that occupational gender segregation is diminishing in some countries (national economies), but persists in others, to different degrees, in different cultures, and at different levels of development.

Redefining gender identities

The feminist struggle for equality is not just about jobs and equal pay. It also challenges male dominance in other domains ranging from the division of household chores to political participation and linguistic representation.

Because we all use language all the time, and because language seems so close to our identity, the gender-neutral language debate gained much attention. Gender identity relates to language in two ways. On the one hand, it is about male and female speech styles, and on the other, about how women and men are represented in written texts and everyday language. This debate originated in the Anglo-Saxon world, where it has led to real changes in the English language. For instance, the use of *he* as a pronoun embracing both genders (generic masculine, like 'the lawyer,... he'), which was normal through the 1970s, has all but disappeared from written English where singular *they* ('someone left their coat in the cloakroom') has become fashionable. (If you think that 'fashionable' is too frivolous a word in this context, think again.)

Proponents of gender-neutral language regulation believe that language does not just consist of arbitrary words and expressions that allow us to say what we want to say, but that it also reflects social realities and makes us see the world in a particular way (for instance that lawyers are men). By exercising an influence on our thinking, however subtle, language use thus reinforces stereotypes that define gender identities. In the same vein, boys and girls learn to follow social norms when they speak. While the instruction 'speak like a lady!' sounds a bit antiquated, communication norms for boys (who 'will be boys') and girls are different and again reinforce stereotypes. Men have more licence to be assertive and rude than women, who are expected to be more polite and modest.

Because gender identities are ensembles of selected personality traits and stereotypes, feminist critics see stylistic guidance that eliminates gender bias as one approach to achieving more social equality.

In English, grammatical gender plays an unimportant role and is, therefore, relatively easy to manipulate. When the gender-neutral debate migrated to other languages, it became clear that the relationship between natural gender and grammatical gender is highly variable. In French, Italian, and Polish, for example, stylistic gender neutrality is more difficult to effect than in English. On the other hand, Hungarian and Chinese along with dozens of other languages have no grammatical gender at all. Many languages have more than two genders, German and Tamil, for example, and many, such as Czech and Danish, have more than three. Swahili has a system of twenty noun classes that fulfil similar functions. What is more, the gender of things and the gender of words denoting them varies across languages. The sun is masculine in Italian, *il sole*, but feminine in German, *die Sonne*. What of that? Shall we lobby for a gender-neutral sun in both languages?

This is perhaps moot, but observations about grammatical gender in different languages must caution us not to jump to conclusions about the relationship between grammatical and social categories.

In the English-speaking world, these considerations had little effect on the gender-neutral language debate, which continues to date, because some feminists are convinced that the perpetuation of linguistic norms and conventions associated with boys and girls reinforce male dominance and make girls develop a stigmatized identity. Other feminists argue that, instead of the cause of gender discrimination, language reform addresses the symptom only and will at best accomplish some window dressing.

If you are committed to equality, it is surely more important to change the world than the language. After all, what's wrong with maintaining distinct styles of speech (dress, hairstyle, conduct, etc.) if these distinctions do not correspond to domination and discrimination? Giving up on sex and gender distinction is not an option because gender is the primary identity any human being holds.

Tertium datur: LGBT

Eradicating discrimination rather than difference is a message that pleases another group (or group of groups) that in recent decades have demanded recognition, the LGBTs, also LGBTQs. The acronym stands for lesbian, gay, bisexual, trans (and queer and questioning), a fuzzy community of people who do not fit the two-valued logic of heterosexual women and men united by the desire not to be subsumed under it. Encouraged by the increasing influence of feminists in research, higher education, and politics, LGBT advocacy groups assert their identity more openly today than they were able to do in the past.

Opposing male dominance within the traditional dualistic gender framework is a defining point of the LGBT agenda, as it is for feminists. However, this does not mean that both always join forces. Initially, feminists were not welcoming of LGBTs for fear of distracting from their main concern of equal rights for women. Conversely, in forming pressure groups, LGBTs often left out (straight) women, perhaps because the range of different concerns and identity issues of gays, lesbians, and others identifying as transgender or non-binary is wide enough in its own right. The desire to safeguard their proper identity may have been an additional motive. Whenever an identity is asserted, more likely than not there will be disagreement as to what it encompasses.

The LGBT agenda benefited from a new anthropology of difference based on genetic research that supports more recognition of fluidity and complexity of sex and gender. The interesting twist here is that while feminists concentrate on socio-cultural gender roles, LGBTs have brought biological sex determination and differentiation back into the discussion. Typically, the sex-determining chromosomes are 46XX for women and 46XY for men, but some individuals are born with other chromosome configurations (single or multiple sex chromosomes).

These natural differences, LGBT persons maintain, should not be glossed over by just focusing on occupational segregation and other cultural practices. In many Western countries the lobbying for LGBT identity rights produced substantial social change, in education, in the military, and perhaps most remarkably, in regards to the institution of marriage (Table 1).

Table 1. Countries where same-sex marriage was legal in 2018.

Country	Legal since
Netherlands	2000
Belgium	2003
Canada, Spain	2005
South Africa	2006
Norway	2008
Sweden	2009
Portugal, Iceland, Argentina	2010
Denmark	2012
New Zealand, France, England, Wales, Brazil, Uruguay	2013
Scotland, Luxembourg	2014
Ireland, Finland, United States	2015
Colombia	2016
Germany, Malta, Australia	2017

Legalizing same-sex marriage and thus redefining a central institution of society indeed is a major change. To LGBTs, it means recognition of their identity, while their opponents see in it an attack on theirs.

The resistance against same-sex marriage, for instance on the part of the Christian Right in the United States and Muslim leaders across Australia, directs our attention to the explosive potential of identity recognition and assertion. In regards to gender as in other fields, it involves power and is often contentious and highly emotional. A horrid manifestation of this was the 2016 mass shooting in a dance club in Orlando, Florida, where forty-nine people were killed for openly living their gay identity.

Conclusions

Like race, gender seems to be an immutable element of our identity, while in both cases natural and socio-cultural determinants interact. In Western societies, gender identities are being renegotiated. The ongoing process was initiated by the Women's Liberation Movement. It exemplifies the fact that gender roles are subject to social norms, political power conditions, and economic exigencies, and as such they are at times controversial. Inside (we) and outside (they) perceptions of identity are not always congruent. The present transformation of gender identities is not limited to women's and men's definitions of femininity and masculinity, but also involves recognition of LGBTs who do not fit a two-valued logic of human sexuality. Modifications of established gender relations are likely to induce discrimination, both in the sense of further sub-divisions and intolerance.

Chapter 5
Identity in politics: promises and dangers

From sex to politics is not a long way, and identity is not the only bridge connecting one with the other; but this is our focus here. For the Women's Rights Movement was an early example of identity politics, a kind of politics centred on the idea of stressing group coherence, collective identity, and separatism. Identity politics is organized by a group and designed to promote its interests. It requires sharp boundaries between groups separated from each other by their mutually exclusive identities. Identities that have been instrumentalized for this purpose include ethnic, religious, linguistic, and ideological allegiances. Overarching all of them, but integrating them not always benignly, is nationalism. Actually, a great deal of contemporary politics is grounded upon tensions between discordant forms of identity within the nation state. But what is a nation state?

The self of politics

In 1866, Friedrich Engels wrote an article about the partition of Poland in which he discussed the 'principle of nationalities' which, he argued, must not be confused with the question of the existence of European nations. It was an important question because at the time there was no state in Europe that did not encompass multiple nationalities. Engels mentions the Highland Gaels, the Welsh, and the Celtic inhabitants of Brittany, among several others that, in his opinion, had no claim to statehood. His article reads surprisingly modern, although, in his days, the present system of European nation states was still in its infancy. Tensions between nations and nationalities (or call them 'macro- and micro-nations') were visible then as they are now.

From a historical point of view, these tensions are a legacy of the dissolution of the great multiethnic empires—the Ottoman, Hapsburg, and Czarist realms—and the principle of self-determination espoused after World War I by the leader of the Russian Revolution, Vladimir Lenin, and US President Woodrow Wilson. A second wave of calls for self-determination came with decolonization where the key issue was liberation from white rule.

The principle of self-determination was hailed as a victory over autocratic domination and an important step in the direction of democratic government, but it is based on a fiction, the fiction of a collectivity of human beings that by virtue of being distinguishable from other such collectivities is able to auto-determine its political fate. Collectivities of this sort are called 'peoples' or 'nations'. Unless you believe in their existence, unless you know that *we* can be distinguished from *them*, you cannot reasonably invoke the principle of self-determination. *Imagined Communities*, the title of an influential book by Benedict Andersen (an Anglo/Irish, China-born, California- and Ireland-raised, UK-USA educated specialist in Indonesian, Philippine, and Thai politics and culture who had three nationalities, British, US, and Irish), therefore became a standard expression in political science to capture the created and fluid as opposed to the given and invariable nature of national communities.

Of course, imagination is not fact. In the world of politics it can help to create facts, that is, communities and identities; which implies that these facts could have been imagined differently. The birth defect of the principle of self-determination is that it fails to say what the *self* might be that would or should determine its own fate. The principle was proclaimed in the absence of any guidelines for drawing a distinction between *nation* and *nationality*, sowing the seeds of disputes. As the experience of the last century teaches, this distinction, if it exists, is subject to fuzzy logic rather than the classical two-valued logic of the excluded middle. How else could we explain the fact that in the course of the 20th century the number of independent states more than tripled? With regard to creating new states in the context of decolonization, the principle of self-determination seemed quite clear: freedom from external domination. However, what it implies for dismembering existing states that look back on a long history, which supposedly is the bedrock of national consciousness (identity), is less obvious. Internal autonomy in terms of language, culture, and administration is one option, secession another. Whether other criteria than sovereignty distinguish nationalities from nations remains an open question. The identity of the collective self is often a point of contention, which is why the politics of identity is a major source of conflict in our time.

Number of independent states, 1917: 59.
Number of independent states, 2017: 195.

To mention just one recent example, strong forces in Catalonia seek independence, while the government in Madrid insists that the Autonomous Community of Catalonia is an inalienable part of the Kingdom of Spain. In the regional election of 2017, the Catalans were nearly split down the middle between advocates and opponents of an independent Catalonia, with a slight majority of separatists. The opponents can imagine a multi-layered identity for themselves, for example, as Barcelonan, Catalan, Spanish, and European; the separatists do not want to live with that. Immediately after the election, an anti-independence movement took shape in Catalonia's southern province Tarragona, offering a presentiment of what an independent Catalonia could expect: further secessions of ever-smaller units.

This is not to say that there are no oppressed nationalities with genuine grievances. The Palestinians come to mind, whose claim to self-determination Israel denies in spite of repeated reconfirmations on the part of the Israeli government that the Palestinians have this right. Kurdistan, Tibet, and Abkhazia are other regions that form part of a state or states from which many of their people wish to secede. Self-determination is a principle of international law which the said communities invariably invoke; but its meaning and the definition of the units to which it might apply remain imprecise.

What, then, is a nation? Two oft-cited positions are the romantic and the republican definitions. The romantic position, associated with German philosophers Johann Gottfried Herder (1747–1803) and Johann Gottlieb Fichte (1762–1814), conceptualizes the nation as age-old heritage rooted in culture, custom, and above all language, in short, in a quasi-natural continuous self-sameness or identity. In contrast, representing the republican position, French historian Ernest Renan (1823–92) characterized the nation as 'a daily plebiscite'. He opposed the notion of race or language as the basis of a nation and instead emphasized the will of a people to live together and shape their future rather than their remembrance of a 'glorious' past. While these two positions look quite different, they are both compatible with the less idealistic notion advanced by sociologist Norbert Elias, who posited that nations were born in wars and for wars. Identities in politics are similarly born in and for confrontation.

Globalization and cultural identity

Fired by nationalism, modern wars were fought by countries. After the dust of World War II had settled, an era of proxy wars began. It lasted until the Berlin Wall came down in 1989, an event that symbolized the end of the Cold War that was defined by ideological fault lines more than by national borders. At the same time, globalization became a reality for a growing part of the world population, not rendering states irrelevant, but reducing their power to shape the future. While nationalism did not disappear from the political landscape and in some parts of the world even resurged, notably in post-Soviet Eastern Europe, other anchors of collective identity formation gained more prominence in the political arena. In domestic politics ethnic identity re-emerged as a major factor, as we saw in Chapter 4, and in global politics the struggle for cultural identity replaced the ideological East–West rivalry (the competition of systems).

This is what political scientist Samuel Huntington argued in his 1996 book *The Clash of Civilizations*. After leading the world for five centuries, the global influence of the West is on the wane, and others are reasserting their cultural identities. The victory of market liberalism over socialism has not, as promised or at least hoped, delivered a peaceful world in which all agree on the values, norms, and common future objectives of humankind. Instead, cultural identities proved to be more long-lived and more important to people's lives than political ideologies, providing today a potent motive for rivalry and conflict.

Asia in particular, with countries as diverse as Japan, China, South Korea, and Singapore in the lead, has driven this process forward. The new Asia is no longer the caricature that Western Orientalism drew of it, but the continent of growth, home to industrial and high-tech giants that proved to the world that modernization could no longer be equated with Westernization. Other civilizations can hold their own.

Against the backdrop of developments that impinge on the lives of common people, such as novel technologies and mass migration, to mention but two conspicuous examples, a sense of insecurity spread through the Western world. The Western values and ideals that in the modern world gave everybody a sense of direction began to erode as material wealth in many postcolonial countries increased, and in the postmodern world these values no longer delineate the only route to a better life. Other identities, understood as ways of life, morals, and political philosophies, which seemed to be destined to ultimate decay until recently (at least from a Western point of view), now constitute alternative templates to understand the world and act on it politically.

This new perspective involves an apparent contradiction. Hybridization is a feature of postmodern life and thought. Boundaries between ethnicities, races, nationalities, faiths, and languages are increasingly seen to be constructed and therefore fluid and moveable. At the same time, the idea of a *clash* of civilizations suggests the existence of solid entities that collide. By reifying civilizations—he distinguishes the following nine: Western, Latin American, African, Islamic, Sinic, Hindu, Orthodox, Buddhist, and Japanese—Huntington laid himself open to criticism. For there is much overlap and interaction between civilizations. Japanese civilization partakes of Sinic and Buddhist civilization; Latin American is hardly wholly distinct from Western civilization; Orthodox and Western civilizations are deeply intertwined, for instance in Greece. Boundaries *are* porous and fluid. Assuming that the civilizational partitioning of the world is a hard fact bears, like identity politics on lower levels, the risk of overgeneralization and what Nobel laureate Amartya Sen calls 'the illusion of destiny'.

Constructivism may offer a way out. In this view, cultural identities are not fixed once and for all but are a source from which to draw to assure one's own position whenever opportune. Confucianism in China is a pertinent example. For much of the 20th century, Chinese intellectuals and politicians condemned it for impeding China's modernization, especially the Communist Party. But when the People's Republic initiated radical economic reforms in the 1980s, Confucianism experienced a renaissance as an important reference point for Chinese identity. Even government officials acknowledged Confucius proudly as a contributor to China's cultural heritage, which in the event dates back 2,500 years and spreads far beyond China's borders, and in this sense underlies a civilizational identity rather than a national identity.

Like his colleagues Gautama Buddha, Jesus Christ, Muhammad, and some others, Confucius stands forever ready to be re-enlisted for supporting claims to civilization identities, which nowadays once again compete with national identities in shaping patterns of cohesion and conflict. Islam, too, exemplifies this tendency, which is the result of an interactive process of how it is portrayed in the Western world and how it functions as a reinvigorated source of identity across national borders, from Morocco to Indonesia. Many internal differences and rivalries between Islamic-majority countries notwithstanding, the same countries often act in unison on the international stage, while many in Europe and the United States perceive a Muslim threat, however ill defined, and take measures to counter it.

Democracy and the identity discourse

The two faces of identity politics become visible here, *our* identity and *your* identity as *we* and *you* construct them for ourselves and mutually. Whatever criteria are used in the process, stereotyping is inevitable and likely to produce much misunderstanding. In high-income countries, this is particularly problematic, as many immigrant groups have adopted the Western notion of identity and with it an ethnic claim to difference. Politically the movability of identities across national borders raises the question of who should be in charge of managing the inevitable structural changes of society, the natives or the newcomers.

Identity politics makes this look like an either–or alternative, partly because the idea of the nation state still holds sway over the political organization of the world and our understanding of it. It implies exclusionism, that is, a sharp line between those who belong and those who do not, those who have the right to determine the identity of a place and those who should accept it, adapt to it, or leave. Recognizing a new (ethnic, religious, gender, linguistic) identity thus becomes a controversial issue of national and local politics. For democracies it poses a dilemma, for the imperative of equal rights for all is hard to reconcile with asserting my identity while denying yours.

This dilemma is rooted in the very notion of identity. Having a collective identity is different from indulging certain tastes, having preferences, speaking one language better than another, and allying oneself with one religious tradition rather than another. Identity is not seen as a matter of choice. Those who emphasize identity rarely acknowledge its constructed and thus adaptable nature, but consider identity as non-negotiable, something that defines the group one belongs to as much as oneself. In the political arena, identity arguments are often presented as irreducible 'reasons' for defending a position: 'Because we are Xs, we (should) have the right to (not) do Y.' Questioning the rationality of such a position is difficult; for when your identity is at stake, nobody can expect you to give in.

The conceptual mistake is to treat the meaning of the term 'identity' as if it were the same in referring to individuals and to groups. This is not nitpicking about semantics. At issue is the danger of undue generalization and discrimination. Because of this confusion and because identity arguments appeal to emotions, they are not falsifiable. Identity arguments have two complementary parts, *'we* are different' and *'you* are different', which makes it all but impossible to evade them. If you insist on having an identity, I cannot easily say, 'I can do without one'.

Justin Trudeau tried to do just that, spelling out an antidote to exclusionist identity politics. After becoming prime minister in 2015, he declared that Canada would be the first 'post-national state'. 'There is no core identity, no mainstream in Canada', he said. This is an ambitious policy statement. In the neighbouring

9. Identity politics?

US, like Canada an immigrant country, a similar statement
would be unlikely to fall on fertile ground (Figure 9). Too deeply
entrenched is the idea that one has to attach oneself to a group
identity to counteract individualism and total isolation in the
globalized world.

Yet some critics consider the insistence on identity in politics to be
a serious problem. For instance, Canadian political philosophers
Daniel Weinstock and his French colleague Pierre Rosanvallon
argue that identity politics is incompatible with, and a danger to,
deliberative democracy. By magnifying differences, it closes the
door to compromise and destroys the *we* a democratic society
ideally should be. The ideals of the French Revolution, *liberté,*

égalité, fraternité and the willingness to overcome differences are sacrificed on the altar of identity assertion. The unacknowledged model of exclusionist identity politics is apartheid, the racial segregation of erstwhile South Africa. The *identitarian movement* embodies similar ideas in a new key. Launched with the formation in 2003 of the *Bloc Identitaire* in France, this movement spread to other European countries and across the Atlantic. It stands for restricting immigration, correcting the presumed preferential treatment of asylum seekers, and upholding native traditions. Since 'identity' has for many a positive ring to it, the identitarian movement chose its name cleverly to give its nationalist, xenophobic, and racist agenda a respectable label.

However, it must also be noted that many people surely find the cultivation and preservation of their cultural heritage, at home or abroad, a noble cause which they do not associate with a rightist intolerant stance. On the contrary, to strengthen the voices of marginalized groups that are mostly drowned out by the majority thus helping them to be treated fairly is more of a left-wing concern. Is then identity politics for and by minorities good and identity politics for and by majorities bad? If only things were that simple!

To its advocates, identity politics is a strategy to overcome repression and achieve social, political, and economic equality, while its opponents consider it an aberration that undermines democracy itself. In pluralistic democracies of the northern hemisphere identity politics plays an increasingly important role, reflecting a common desire to find shelter from the disruptions of globalization by belonging to a group of likeminded people with shared interests and objectives. The democratic process consists not just of the relation between voters and their elected representatives, but involves an interplay of constituencies, political parties, lobbies, alliances of convenience, and identity groups. If recent developments in Western democracies are any indication, the proclivity of identity politics is increasing.

Whether identity politics is good or bad, whether it is an illicit deviation from the principle of majority rule or a prerequisite of equality, depends on one's views. However, it is uncontroversial that identity politics presents a challenge to pluralistic democracies that get more pluralistic with continuing migration flows. Some of the pressing questions facing the development of democratic systems today thus have to do with identity politics:

How is a democracy to distinguish groups that advance justice and equality from groups that pursue supremacy and undermine the common good of freely elected democratic rule?

How is identity politics different from special interest politics—e.g. environmentalists vs private sector industrialists?

Should identity politics be allowed to exempt members of certain minorities from observing established and widely accepted rules?

Is identity politics compatible with multiculturalism, cosmopolitanism, and ecumenism?

These questions, among others, relate to the relationship between the individual and groups in democratic societies. The imperative of equality before the law and in the political process puts the individual at the centre. The ballot box is the principal mechanism to mediate interests and determine policies. This ideal could perhaps work in a perfectly homogeneous nation state; however, in many democratic countries the internal diversity has produced and perpetuated structural disadvantages for racial, ethnic, gender, and religious groups. Originally, identity politics was a response to the inability to reconcile diversity with equality. Though motivated by the emancipatory intent to combat discrimination, it was met by an identity politics of a different kind, one that flies the flag of excluding and demonizing the Other.

The present-day question about identity in politics then is this: what role should and will identity politics play in the future development of pluralistic democracies?

Conclusions

Identity in politics is thus a challenge to democratic rule rooted in the principle of self-determination. As a natural child of nationalism it gives rise to conflicts that political scientists study at multiple levels. At the subnational level, the focus is on ethnicities and other group affiliations and, at the supranational level, they are concerned with civilization identities (e.g. Western, Islamic, Sinic). Considering conflicts in terms of civilization identities is sometimes persuasive, sometimes not, for there is the risk of stereotyping, while identities are historically contingent and can be instrumentalized for political purposes of various kinds. Because identities tend to be presented as non-negotiable, identity politics is hard to reconcile with deliberative democracy as it makes compromise difficult to achieve.

Chapter 6
'Your station in life': social identities in our time

Social stratification

Societies are not amorphous collections of individuals, but structured aggregates in which everyone has a place, a station in life. Since these stations are not allotted or acquired at random, their distribution can be studied. This is the job of sociologists; they investigate inequality. Societies differ in how they are stratified, that is, how inequality is organized, and in terms of the rigidity and possibilities of choice of social categories.

People can be classified according to various systems of partitioning. The sociologist's task is to discover the categories that are pertinent for his/her society and design a model that represents the relevant social divisions. For example, medieval European feudalism was a social order characterized by relatively fixed 'estates' that determined one's life course and the nature of personal relationships between aristocrats and peasant serfs. A similar system obtained in Japan until the mid-19th century where the Samurai elite were at the top followed by farmers, artisans, and at the bottom of the pyramid, merchants. One's station in life (social identity) in such a system was inherited rather than accomplished on the basis of merit. A feudal hierarchy could be more fine-grained, including knights, vassals, merchants, artisans, and a special place for clerics, but there wasn't much question about its stable nature. Social segregation manifested itself in terms of endogamy (marrying neither below nor above (one's) estate), the right to bear arms (or lack thereof), common customs and traditions, food preferences, and dress. Taken together, these features made people's social position visibly recognizable.

The Hindu caste system is another example of a rigid system of hereditary social stratification defined by descent and craft. Although legally abolished in India, by means of the perpetuation of endogamy it continues to play a powerful role in structuring Indian society today, as matrimonial newspaper ads clearly testify (Figure 10). Caste partitions dominate social interaction in many other ways, including housing and employment. Sexual assaults and gang rapes of Dalit (or so-called untouchable) women that occasionally make it into the Western press are particularly frightful expressions of the cruelty of this atavistic system of social stratification.

The industrial revolution transformed the social order of Western societies and with it the identity of many people, turning serfs into factory workers. Social class replaced feudal estate as the most relevant category for describing people's position in society. As a response to these developments, various theories of class were put forth, Karl Marx's and Max Weber's models being most influential. In Marx's view, there were basically two social classes, the bourgeoisie which controlled the means of production, and the workers (the proletariat) who had only their sellable labour force to offer in the market. Weber's model integrated three components of class—wealth, prestige, and power—and related them to the concept of an individual's life chances. Marx believed that workers would eventually realize that, though freed from the bondage of serfdom, they were being exploited and develop a class consciousness, or a sense of shared identity.

BRAHMIN

SUITABLE match for
Punjabi Brahmin Boy 33yrs
5'10" NRI Canada Parents in
Gujarat. M: 09879613673
angrish009@hotmail.com

SM4 July'83 born, B.E MBA,
working in MNC gurgaon, 7 di-
git salary, seeks well educated
girl. Email profile & photo at:
matrimony2783@gmail.com ,
9355272124

PQM4 Pb Srwt br boy
Nov82/176 BTech MBA wrkg
Central Govt Maharatna PSU
Mum 14LPA. Prfr CA/Engr.
Em: kiransh160@gmail.com

SM4 Gaur Br. 1970 Boy never
married. Qlfd wkg rptd intl
NGO,Delhi. Seeks qlfd, cultrd
girl under 36.Not of Kaushik,
Vashisht gotra.#09810459876,
E: rd111kaushik@gmail.com

PQM4 BR 24/01/86, 2:10AM,
Patiala, MCA, working in MNC
Pune, mail: kiransh167@
gmail.com , 9888521671. MNCs
preferred

10. **Matrimonial newspaper ads,** *Hindustan Times***: 'All Brahmins
acceptable'.**

To some extent this happened, as evidenced, for example, by
the coming into existence of Labour Parties, Social Democratic
Parties, and the Socialist International that in the beginning very
much represented a workers' identity. The Socialist *International*
notably challenged nationality as the most general reference plane
of allegiance and identity formation, though to little avail, if we
just remember the great wars of the 20th century that made
workers fight against workers. People were never only workers or
only compatriots or only children, spouses, and parents.
Overlapping, supplementing, and conflicting identities were
always a reality in their lives.

Marx warned against pigeonholing people as members of one social category only. Yet for some time, being a factory worker was a life-determining feature for many that related not just to their workplace and wage, but also to where they lived, how they dressed, whom they married, where their children went to school, etc. Class consciousness there was, circumscribing a kind of social identity.

'Proletariat' was a political notion, whereas 'working class' was usually considered a descriptive category that contrasted with 'upper class', 'middle class', and 'underclass'. In attempts to refine class theory, some studies further subdivided the middle class into lower, middle, and upper middle class. As of the late 1950s, material gains of workers in advanced industrial societies prompted the question, 'Does class matter?'—the title of a five-part BBC documentary TV series in 1958—to stimulate many studies about class, class consciousness, and class identity. Until about the 1970s, the idea of class was convincing enough to shape the public image of Western industrial society and to serve social scientists as an analytic tool.

As consumer capitalism took shape, sociologists proposed new classes, such as the 'managerial class' (no ownership, but control over means of production), 'service workers' (by income and kind of job removed from workers in industrial production), and the 'creative class' (defined by lifestyle and consciousness). Of these new classes, it was not always clear whether they described factual dimensions of social stratification or ideologically informed constructs. In the meantime, the question about class has been answered variously, some sociologists arguing that class divisions still characterize advanced societies, but are today expressed differently than a generation or two ago; others consider class to be an obsolete category. In as much as a class consciousness did develop, it can be said to have shaped many people's identity, but it did not arrest social change. The Enlightenment promise of equality implied the possibility of social mobility, i.e. changing social identities, even under conditions of a rigid division of labour.

Crosscurrents

The past several decades have seen changes whose gravity matches those of the industrial revolution. Previously stable settings and relationships crumbled under the impact of socio-economic developments that transformed the social system. The most consequential changes have been the following.

First, while parts of the working class became more affluent, obscuring the distinction between blue-collar and white-collar work, economic disparities between rich and poor not just continued but widened. Privatization, deregulation, and new forms of employment that made life courses more varied and less predictable drove the individualization of society to new highs, undermining the solidarity of the working class to the extent that it lost its contours.

Second, the rising labour force participation of women reinforced this trend in as much as it contributed to distorting the image of the proletarian worker's identity, which, female and child labour notwithstanding, once was decidedly male. In many instances, more female workers also meant more double-income households, another factor of rising inequality. Lifestyle and consumption patterns came to supersede class as a determiner of social identity.

Third, in the former colonial countries of the West, immigrants from southern parts of the globe filled the space opened up by a vanishing proletariat. As one of the intertwining threads of the fabric of globalization, this process resulted in the *ethnification of social class*. In the United States, slavery had laid the groundwork of a social hierarchy in which race was a central dimension of inequality and where race is still a strong predictor of per capita income—today: White, Asian, Black, Hispanic, in that order. Similar patterns appeared in Western European countries in the wake of decolonization. Nowadays, an ethnic underclass is a common feature in many cities. This is a society where housing rent varies with the tenants' ethnicity, and where your station in life may be a stop on a commuter train; for instance Aulnay-sous-Bois on the Île-de-France Line 4 in Paris, or Thamesmead Town Centre, a stop on the 244 bus line in London, where chances are you will see mostly black people get on and off. In Paris, London, or Brussels, skin colour, place of residence, infant mortality, and per capita income nowadays show significant correlations formerly associated with social class and are hence indicative of new social divisions and identities.

Fourth, level of education (literacy) has always been an important variable of social stratification. With the advent of the digital age and the knowledge society, it became more important than ever, opening up new opportunities of participation in economic life across social classes. Certified skills are still valuable in the marketplace, but at the same time, new ways of making money not dependent on any formal education have emerged in cyberspace. 'Disruptors', who interfere with or destroy normal processes to try out and benefit from some innovation that may or may not be useful, are celebrated as heroes, while educators promote the idea of lifelong learning for many professions. This is a society with reduced continuity and stability, where changing jobs in the course of one's professional life is common and attachments are contingent. Mobile recruiting apps are representative of current trends. People scan job offers, upload their CV and supporting documents, and add a little video clip to flaunt their identity, all while being on the move. They expect to receive an answer on their mobile device and are ready to start work tomorrow or next week, for a week, a month, a year, but hardly for life.

As no one explained more lucidly than Polish-British sociologist Zygmunt Bauman, these developments among some others have as their consequences more fragmentation of social attachments and a growing sense of insecurity. Ties that used to be considered solid are no longer reliable, in the labour market, in particular, but not only there. Individualization worked against class solidarity and debilitated the power of trade unions. Commitments to work and family alike are weakening. With accelerating business cycles, jobs are becoming less permanent, while in OECD countries the population share of those who have always been single and will never marry has risen to an all-time high. The country that has been at the forefront of a labour culture of hire-and-fire, the US, not only has an extremely low unionization rate (e.g. Sweden 82 per cent of the labour force, US 13 per cent), but also the highest divorce rate. This is not coincidental. Both statistics are indicative of the progressing dissolution of social bonds.

From 'identity' to 'identifying with'

We can speak of the identity of aristocrats and of members of other feudal estates or of the identity of the European bourgeoisie in the 19th century. There is nothing wrong with that; but when using such terminology one must be aware that it represents an anachronistic perspective imposed on the object of investigation from our point of view, which is informed by the current obsession with the concept. At the beginning of the industrial age, social identity was not an issue, much less so in feudalism. In the early days of sociology, in the late 19th century, identity was not an important category, in society or analytically. Émile Durkheim contemplated shared moral goals as a prerequisite of collective identity, but other than that, references to identity in early sociological writing were few.

Today, however, we are living in a society of identities. Influential sociologists such as Pierre Bourdieu and Richard Jenkins take the position that socialization and the working of society cannot be explained without reference to collective identities based on shared qualities, however fuzzy, real or imagined. To have a social existence, these identities require difference, counterparts that they are not and from which they set themselves apart. Thus, in contemporary sociology 'identity' is a relational concept that derives from the tension between self-sameness and other-difference, both of which, however, need not be that forever, but, being relational, are constantly under construction and renegotiation.

Ironically, the shift, dissolution, redrawing, and blurring of social categories, the hybridization of jobs, the creolization of ethnicities, the mixing of cultures in multicultural settings have not led to the abandonment of identity as a meaningful social variable. Quite the contrary, everyone must have one, or several. 'Identity' is the talk of the town, especially of the multicultural town, and sociology has to explain why in the second half of the 20th century identity suddenly became a central concern of common and scholarly deliberation.

Part of the problem is that identity is not given quasi-naturally by birth, but is subject to many tugs of war between choosing and imputing, seeking and imposing. In other fields of research discussed earlier, 'Who am I?' and 'Who are we?' are critical questions of identity. In sociology, the question is this: 'Who or what do you *identify with* (and are allowed to do so)?' The concept 'to identify with', originally introduced by Sigmund Freud, functions as a channel connecting the flows of an individual identity with those of a shared social identity.

Identity became an issue when the appropriation of a station in life ceased to be, for increasingly larger parts of the population, determined by birth. This implies options and obligations, the possibility and the necessity to construct an identity for yourself; or several. That people have 'multiple identities' in cyberspace should not be misunderstood as a sloppy allegory. Digital identities connect us in new ways and play an increasingly important role in our day-to-day activities. 'Reinvent yourself!' is an emblematic expression of our age. Such *acts of identity* are both liberating, as children do not have to follow their parents in the professional world, and demanding, as they have to navigate the uncharted sea of social, economic, and cultural crosscurrents to construct their own identity, the principal orientation marks being ads on their smartphones.

The answer lies in seeking membership, a *we* to which you might belong and which alleviates the loneliness of the super-individualistic society: a school, a fan club, a church, a political party, a civic organization, a choir, a fitness centre, and of course a company. Membership in such organizations is often exclusive. Joining the fan club of the Pinks means not joining that of the Blues, and that is a crucial point of the whole operation. Sameness and belonging is to a considerable extent dependent on difference from and rejection of others. Distinction of corporate identity is essential. The easiest way to express it is by dress (Figure 11).

Patterns of social organization are generated through interaction between groups. To this end, it must be possible to hold the relevant groups apart. Imagine a football match where spectators were barred from displaying their allegiance to or sympathy with one of the teams! It would be a different social event. A symbolic

11. **Clothes make the man.**

repertoire of tokens of identity is indispensable; a flag, a sweatshirt, a muffler that enables you to show what you identify with and unites you with your soulmates. You are what you wear, or you are made to wear what ostensibly you are.

Can identities be put on and slipped off like a T-shirt? Roland Barthes, one of the most original observers of the 20th century, knew that the old adage, 'clothes make the man', is still true (never mind the generic masculine). In the 21st century it is even truer, but it means something different. Fashion, Barthes understood, is essentially a modern phenomenon. Not that attire did not change in pre-modern times; but in modernity, fashion performs the paradoxical function of marking both individual distinction and collective community, in short, this season's identity. Join, if you can, be entirely your own self and part of the flock!

Fashion is quintessentially social, mediating individual and community needs. Since Barthes wrote his essay *Système de la Mode* half a century ago, the penetration of consumer capitalism into every sphere of everyday life has caused fashion cycles to shorten considerably. Fast fashion, a business model that reduced the time from production to consumption, is one of the trends that represent the pressure regularly to reconstruct your identity in contemporary society. The individual is given a seemingly endless choice, and yet the outcome is conformity on a large scale. A fashion style quiz, such as 'Quick Test to *Identify* Your *Clothing* Personality', helps you to find out what you want to identify with and differentiate yourself from. The shrinking lifespan of fashion items and the increased currency of the verb 'to identify with' are indicative of current developments of social identity, more precisely, of those aspects of social identity that are open to choice.

The dark side of identity

Sociologists widely agree on the importance of identity in contemporary society. It comes to bear both on the level of society as a whole and on that of its constituent groups, institutions, and associations. After the discussion so far, it is perhaps plausible that a society's identity is best understood as a project rather than a state of affairs. Every society constructs its own identity and perpetuates itself by maintaining and incessantly reconstructing it. Smaller units that integrate individuals as their members partake in this process, creating and recreating their identities that are in harmony or conflict with each other and the overarching national identity. On both levels, identity is a relational process of inclusion and exclusion.

A peaceful society is one in which the level of contestation of both is low, where a fan club T-shirt is not more than that. It can be worn on a Saturday afternoon and put aside after the match. Yet, insignia of collective identity are not always so harmless. Membership as a pretext for pitting one identity against another is a well-known phenomenon, outbursts of hooligan violence just being one example. They alert us to the divisive potential of social identity assertion.

The great challenge of a society that rejects predetermined stations in life as the principal means of giving orientation, security, and comfort is how to offer its members a common purpose they can identify with without denigrating other identities or denying their right to exist. As sociologist Erving Goffman has shown, this is not easy; for collective identities are not just constructed on the inside of a group, but may also be imposed on a group from the outside. A brand, if we recall the origin of the expression, is not just what we want to protect as our own, but also a sign of damnation.

By forming social categories, we impute to individuals certain characteristics and attributes, which taken together constitute in Goffman's terminology a 'virtual social identity' which may concur with or deviate from their 'actual social identity', i.e. the ensemble of characteristics and attributes these individuals actually possess. A wide discrepancy between virtual and actual social identity amounts to a stigma.

Stigmatization reduces individuals with a multiplicity of characteristics to the categories we have available for them: (just a) foreigner, homosexual, Black, Jew, Muslim, illegal immigrant, beggar, etc. Stigmas are characteristics that are socially devalued and used to ostracize, marginalize, and in the extreme case dehumanize groups. They make for imputed, humiliating virtual social identities that in the name of the presumed common good of the integrated identity of the wider society often meet with grave intolerance. This is where the normative expectation to integrate, to blend in, to defer to the identity of the majority reveals its perils. Under the impression of the holocaust, the philosopher Theodor W. Adorno accordingly argued that genocide is the absolute integration legitimized by the ideology of identity.

Today, few social scientists would roundly condemn social identities or dispute the necessity of integrating the various composite parts of a society to make them identify with the whole (a political objective currently known as 'diversity management'). This, however, cannot distract from the fact that the stigmatization of virtual social identities is a perennial danger threatening the weak.

Stigmas are of two kinds, visible and invisible. Both have profound effects on the lives of those concerned. Skin colour, physical disabilities, and age are obvious examples of visible stigmas, which typically, much as they would like, people cannot conceal. Invisible stigmas include mental illness, being LGBT, and one's family background. Because of socially indexed residential patterns of segregation, people may also hesitate to tell others of where they live. Loïc Wacquant, a specialist in urban sociology, therefore speaks of 'territorial stigmatization'. Living in the ghetto/shanty town/slum is doubly debilitating, physically tough, and socially damaging.

Overgeneralization, reduction, and demonization are the hallmarks of stigmatization. Visible stigmas make discrimination easy, and the affected individuals are particularly vulnerable. We can see now how the ostensibly harmless principle *you are what you wear* is a Janus-faced social practice that separates social groups, for good or ill. Differences in dress, be it single items of apparel or whole outfits, are deliberately employed to reinforce group boundaries, but when a skullcap is enough to harm even small children, the dangers of openly displaying a minority group identity are obvious and may lead to the irrepressible desire to conceal it.

Attire that is identified with a social group sometimes serves as a catalyst of conflict. The 2016 controversy about the ban by some French municipalities of full-body swimwear (burkini) on beaches and the outlawing by some countries of face-covering (burqa) in public are recent examples. They also illustrate the difficulties hybrid identities present to societies that are committed to individual liberty but have long taken a level of homogeneity for granted that visible displays of distinction seem to challenge.

Conclusions

Social identity, then, is to do with membership in groups that are horizontally and vertically structured, internally and in relation to each other. Taken together these groupings constitute a society. In industrial society, education, work, and income used to be the major determinants of social identity. With the growth of the service sector, class divisions started to become less distinct and were at the same time supplemented, if not superseded, by ethnic divisions. Consequently, the general understanding of social class is changing, but since economic inequality not only persists but rises, the issue of social stratification and identity remains topical. Group identities are relational, resulting from the inclusion of peers and the exclusion of others. Reducing individuals to a single identity as members of a group amounts to discrimination and stigmatization.

Chapter 7

Citizenship, legal status, and proof of identity: identity as a legal concept

Legal identity

The *natural person* is a core pillar of the present world order, which is grounded upon normative universal principles, such as Article 1 of the Universal Declaration of Human Rights (UDHR): 'All human beings are born free and equal in dignity and rights.' Jurists interpret this article as meaning that every human being has a legal personality with rights and duties. Historically this was not always so. In some pre-modern societies, slaves and serfs were denied 'dignity and rights', being considered objects rather than persons.

The idea that personal autonomy and self-identity are inalienable features of all human beings took time to be universally accepted. Especially in regards to children it has been necessary explicitly to affirm their personal autonomy and individual identity; for they are unable to sustain themselves and depend on their parents, who are required (morally or legally) to provide for them and are responsible for their actions. Because this should not imply that children are deprived of identity, building on an earlier declaration of the League of Nations, the UN in 1989 adopted the Convention on the Rights of the Child. Its Article 7 stipulates that a child is entitled to have a legal identity by being registered, to have a name and a nationality.

International law recognizes the right to a personal identity and the obligation to have one. In modern societies this is taken for granted, but it is worth noting that these stipulations represent a contingent form of social organization and still have not been implemented universally. The European Network on Statelessness estimates the number of stateless persons worldwide at more than 15 million. For all states committed to UDHR Article 1, these persons represent legal and moral difficulties, because, for the conditions of Article 7 of the Convention on the Rights of the Child to hold comprehensively, borders are indispensable—borders separating individuals and borders separating states.

These borders define the relations between citizen and state. The point of departure is the assumption of autonomous individuals who can be distinguished one from another. Their identity is indicated and certified by a personal name (or legal name) that refers to one individual. As a matter of principle, personal names should single out one and only one individual from the whole set of citizens. In reality, this is not always the case, witness John Smith.

Most countries have a name law regulating family names, the naming of married couples, the gender of forenames, the names of children born in and out of wedlock, and in some cases, what first names may be used. Names have a strong link to their bearers' identities, like trademarks that have to be registered for ownership to be secured. Changing one's name is difficult and will not be effected without a legal deed. Only with a name will you be recognized as having rights and obligations. You are not free to call yourself John today and Mary tomorrow or to decide henceforth to go through life without a name; for without a name you have no identity, in the legal sense of the word. Dissociating your legal name from your writer's name by using a pseudonym has legal implications, too. If a writer does not make it known to the publisher that he/she is using a pseudonym, this will be a breach of contract, and the author's copyright may be affected. What is more, if you do not register a trademark for your pseudonym, others may use it.

Legal codes define rights, duties, and other legal characteristics for 'normal persons' who can be identified unmistakably. Only normal persons enjoy the privileges offered by the law and can be expected to abide by the law. Statutory registers for birth, death, marriage, guardianship, adoption, gender recognition, etc. assume and require the unambiguous identity of those registered. Similarly, the law assumes that the parties to registered contracts, land ownership, and litigation can be identified without difficulty. Without these and some other assumptions, the legal structure of the state would collapse. Every legal system defines its own applicability and assumes, explicitly or implicitly, that those to whom it does and does not apply can be identified and separated from one another.

Citizenship

The rule of law presupposes a clearly defined concept of citizenship, which in turn presupposes an unmistakable identity for everyone. In a modern state, one's life extends from birth certificate to death certificate. Countries, therefore, have citizenship laws delimiting their membership boundaries by specifying the conditions of having and obtaining nationality or citizenship. *Jus sanguinis* (right of blood) determines a person's nationality on the basis of their (one or both) parents' nationality, whereas *jus soli* (right of soil or birthright) grants nationality to anyone born in the state territory. These are two common principles informing in various ways the world's citizenship laws. Both principles imply that the vast majority of all people acquire citizenship by accidental circumstances of birth. UDHR Article 1 does not entitle you to any citizenship. Canadian jurist Ayelet Shachar, therefore, speaks of the 'birthright lottery' and argues that, because they restrict free movement, citizenship laws are a major mechanism of perpetuating global inequality.

Citizenship allows you to live in a country, send your children to school there, benefit from the healthcare system, and enjoy other forms of social protection. It may also involve obligations, such as paying taxes, being loyal to the constitution, and defending the nation. The balance of profit and loss for a country's citizenship varies drastically across nations, but when it comes to allotting membership in a state, there is no way around the arbitrary principles of blood-and-soil; unless you are very wealthy and ready to pay for or invest in an additional (national) identity.

The fact that the world of nation states is unequal finds expression in quality rankings of citizenships and the price tag of identity papers. The best passports are those that allow for uninhibited travel to the most countries. They are highly coveted and, in some cases, officially for sale. Famously, Malta, the smallest member state of the EU and always strapped for cash, sells its citizenship for €650,000, a spouse getting almost a free ride for a paltry additional €25,000. Several other countries offer passports to those who are willing to invest in business or real estate.

Programmes of this sort are not for the needy, and they show that hallowed principles sanctioned by law—territory, descent—need not get in the way of big plans when you get the equation right. Selling and buying forged passports is another line of business, which, because of the value disparity of different citizenships, is quite lucrative for the entrepreneurs, although falsifying has become a high-tech operation.

It was only in the early 20th century that passports assumed their present-day functions as proof of identity and means of immigration control. As a result, the words 'identity' and 'identify' have acquired a bureaucratic savour. The evolution of passports and other ID documents well illustrates the progress of the all-encompassing state that assigns a place to every citizen and keeps the alien out. In the course of the 20th century, this became a preoccupation of the welfare state, so much so that passports that once were simple sheets of paper certifying their bearer's name and address, perhaps mentioning eye colour and height, with an official stamp or seal, have become as difficult to counterfeit as legal tender. Because so much depends not just on being who you are, but on being able to prove it, the technology of forgery-proofing identity documents has become very sophisticated. Nowadays ID documents include security features such as biometric photographs, bidimensional barcodes, microchips with fingerprints and iris patterns, holograms, and watermarks.

Identity cards (also identification cards) serve the purpose to unequivocally identify the individual citizen and to protect this citizenship against interlopers. Many people resent the idea of making identity cards compulsory as violating individual privacy, but the majority of countries have done so, and the grid with which individuals are identified and classified is becoming finer and finer. Travelling legally across international borders without an identity card or passport has become all but impossible, while most states continue to refine their tools for registering citizens, assigning them a digital identity that can be verified with the scan of a fingerprint or an iris photograph. In one of the biggest projects of this sort ever, India has recorded these data of all 1.3 billion Indian citizens. This identity programme, called Aadhaar, or 'foundation', is designed to bring digital identity proof to the poor and facilitate access to welfare benefits, while at the same time reducing waste by eliminating 'ghosts' and duplicates. A digital identity thus will become indispensable in India, as doubtless it will elsewhere. The United Nations has declared that one of its goals is to provide everybody on earth with a legal identity by 2030.

Failing the normality test

The rule of law must assume that the population consists of subsistent unique individuals, normal persons with a name and distinct from all others. This is the foundation of how the law understands human identity. The superstructure of human rights rests on this notion. But what is a normal person? The assumption of normalcy itself generates new categories of human beings, those that fail the normality test. Here are some examples.

Identical twins are not normal persons in the legal sense. After a spectacular heist in a department store in Berlin, the police tracked down the perpetrator based on DNA traces found at the scene of the crime, but he went free. The reason: he had an identical twin. In court, the police could prove at least one of the brothers broke into the department store, but were unable to determine which one.

Dead people are not normal persons in the legal sense, or are they? Deceased persons need to file income tax returns. Deceased persons may receive dividends and pensions (which next of kin have occasionally been reported to collect, for instance in super-high life expectancy Japan). And we haven't even touched on the delicate question of how dead a person has to be to count as dead. Of late—meaning a few decades—'loss of personhood' has become the subject of intense and difficult deliberations about the death of human beings. 'Loss of personhood' is another word for brain death, a concept that has changed our thinking about the border between life and death. Can it be equated with the extinction of someone's identity? Hardly, because a deceased person's physical identity persists and can be relevant, for instance to prove their innocence or guilt post-mortem.

Demented people are not normal persons. When do forgetfulness, nominal amnesia, and lack of self-awareness fade into irreversible attenuation of personality? Does a change of personality imply a change of a person's identity? The capacity to bequeath one's property by will presupposes soundness of mind. Can we really measure that soundness? How many wills have been contested for lack of testamentary capacity?

Schizophrenics are not normal persons. When destructive antisocial acts are committed, mental illness may be, but is not always, recognized as extenuating circumstance reducing the perpetrator's culpability. As in other cases, such as voluntary intoxication and drug addiction, where lawyers plead diminished responsibility, the court has to deal with a continuum of culpability. This raises the question of capacity, that is, a person's ability to make decisions for him or herself. Particularly problematic are patients exhibiting dissociative identity disorder, as they call into question the unqualified validity of the notion of a unified unchanging self that inhibits its body for its lifetime.

Undocumented foreigners and *illegal aliens* are not normal persons. It is not so much a symbolic act when asylum seekers discard or destroy their passports and other identity papers; some do it to make it more difficult for the government of the target country to deport them. And it *is* difficult for governments to deal with people who have no identity, no matter activists' justified argument that human beings cannot be illegal and one's identity cannot depend on a registration number.

Witnesses who testified to a crime and have subsequently received in a witness protection programme a new identity and background to safeguard their security are not normal persons.

Someone who has the same name as a convict or disgraced individual is not a normal person. When you are targeted by a flood of hate mail referring to whatever crime or misconduct your namesake is accused of it becomes apparent how unpleasant and disquieting matters of mistaken identity can be.

A thief who uses someone else's identity is not a normal person. Most states make it a crime to misuse another person's identifying information. This fact alone is indicative of the paramount legal importance of identity, that is, the verified self-sameness of a human being. Digitalization has rendered identity theft one of the most common and profitable crimes, making governments around the world struggle to get a grip on it.

Other types of non-normal persons could be added to this list, but for our purpose, it shall be sufficient. When a stranger comes into contact with the judiciary, or a demented person, or identical twins, or impostors, their attributes coalesce to form an atypical identity that poses a challenge to a system built for normal persons capable of assuming obligations and holding rights. Personal identity in the judicial sense is a highly abstract notion, a normative principle from which reality often deviates. Every one of us is a token of the ideal type 'normal person', and none of these tokens is perfect. Each and every one is flawed in one way or another. For the purposes of the law, the difficult task is to define, or decide on a case-by-case basis, what level of flawedness is compatible with the capacity to access the civil and juridical system and, in particular, the ability to sue and be sued. All legal acts presuppose the capacity and the distinctive personal identity of those involved. At times, both are hard to establish.

Forensic identification

In 2013, scientists of the University of Leicester identified Richard III, 'beyond reasonable doubt'. Richard was not on a most wanted list; he died in battle more than 500 years ago. Yet the scientific analysis of his remains was a feat of forensic identification. The evidence presented in the case includes data of various kind, notably DNA and radiological analysis, radiocarbon dating, and anatomical information. This opens up new perspectives for historical research and is of great interest to several fields of law.

Concealing or altering the agent's identity or that of the victim is part of many crime schemes. Forensic identification science is the discipline that develops the methods and theories to unravel the ensuing mysteries. It makes use of all available techniques relating to identity on national, social, ethnic, psychological, linguistic, and genetic levels. Typically, forensic expert testimony presented in court leans on the principle of the identity of indiscernibles (Leibniz's Law, introduced in Chapter 2), for lawyers appreciate clearness. The assumption is that two indistinguishable items—for example, blood or saliva samples—can only have been produced by the same agent.

Conventional forensic identification techniques include methods of analysing blood, semen, fingerprints, palm prints, hair, bite marks, handwriting, as well as facial recognition and voice recognition. But these techniques may not definitively resolve a good whodunit. None of them is foolproof, as indicated by numerous cases of convicts who were exonerated by new means of forensic identification not available at the time of their trial. Even fingerprints, for a long time the epitome of unmistakable identity proof, have on occasion led to erroneous identification and conviction.

Novel identification techniques include *forensic genetics* (DNA typing) and *digital identity tracking* (network user monitoring), which represent real advances in forensic science. A theoretically interesting aspect of these techniques is that they do not rely on Leibniz's Law, but represent probabilistic approaches to identification, incorporating data in quantitative rather than qualitative form.

DNA analysis still does not resolve the identical twin problem, but the data-based probabilistic identity assessment offered by DNA typing provides more reliable evidence that two samples of a substance came from the same source than Leibnizian binary decisions of match or no match. The use of DNA evidence in court is bound to increase and have an effect on the conceptualization of personal identity in law.

Digital identity tracking makes use of methods that evolved in response to the spread of digital technologies and distribution of networks. The prototype of network tracking are 'cookies' that record internet surfers' tastes. However, by the standards of development speed of digital technology, cookies come from the Middle Ages. State-of-the-art tracking is about metadata that expose habits, work schedules, affiliations, and political and religious attachments, among many others, making customers, citizens, supporters, and enemies of the regime not just traceable, but entirely transparent. Metadata allow websites and those who exploit them for their purposes to track the 'fingerprints' of digital devices. For instance, it is possible to retrieve from the browser that you/your device uses a complete list of all fonts and extensions you have ever installed. In combination with the online trace you inevitably leave behind when surfing from one website to another, the tracker is able to construct a very informative profile of you, a dossier or 'pseudo identity' in digitalese, without ever having met you.

'Pseudo identity' is an emblematic concept of the age of big data. This is the age of selling and stealing personal data. It's the age of China's Social Credit System and the National Security Agency cooperating with Google and Facebook; the age of eiC (electronic identification card), eIDV (electronic identity verification), IMS (International Mobile Subscriber Identity), and CIU (compulsive internet use). The satellite navigation systems GPS, Russia's GLONASS, China's BeiDou, and Europe's Galileo have been indispensable for some time already, while RFID (radio-frequency identification) for persons is up and coming. This is a technology used in microchips implanted under your skin, which enables you to communicate with devices such as secured doors, vending machines, etc., without remembering a code, by holding your hand near them. The microchips can also contain various kinds of personal information, such as demographic data, medical history, allergies, credit score, etc. A Swedish company began implanting, on a voluntary basis, workers with RFID chips in 2015. Remote surveillance is 'not intended'. However, the use of these and many other devices generates data, and the question remains what happens to it, who is licenced to use it, and who uses it without licence.

CIU is pathological, but being connected has become so essential that a human right of internet access is being seriously discussed. To the 'digital natives' it is a fixture, a part of their identity. They touch their smartphone—and who does not have one!—more than 1,000 times a day on average. There is in this range of experience of personalized algorithms and electronic devices to connect a quality that adds an element to our identity as legal subjects and as social beings. As digitalization progresses, our pseudo identity merges with our identity, if only because it includes information about the people we connect with and about our whereabouts on this planet. We cannot run away from it, which is why Glenn Greenwald entitled his book about former National Security Agency contractor Edward Snowden's quixotic attempt to shed some light into the dark side of this brave world of ours, *No Place to Hide*.

Conclusions

Individual identity is the cornerstone of the rule of law and the relationship between state and citizen. In law, it has to do with that which makes a person (or thing) distinct from any other person (or thing). It means that a subject is the same as it claims, or is charged, to be. The digital turn has added a new aspect to our legal identity, and protecting us against identity theft is a new obligation of the state, while we have no choice but learn to protect ourselves against profit-seeking corporations, on the one hand, and a surveillance state, on the other.

Chapter 8
Selfhood and personality: the psychology of identity

A sense of self

Philosophy tries to answer the question 'Who am I?' from a general point of view of metaphysics and epistemology. Psychology relates the same question to people with thoughts and emotions who are growing up and living in a specific place, entertaining basic values, relating to other members of society, and having to position themselves in it. As they grow up, they become competent members of their society by forming an individual identity recognized by others and themselves.

Ever since Sigmund Freud in the early 20th century advanced his psychosexual theory of personality development, we know that this is a delicate process. The model Freud devised to conceptualize the human psyche as it unfolds from dependent newborn to autonomous adult turned out to be one of the most influential contributions to psychology ever. In this model, personal identity is structured into three parts, the id, the ego (or *I*), and the superego (or *above I*). These are interacting systems playing different roles at different stages of development.

The id consists of the innate instinctual drives underlying sexual desire and aggressiveness. The superego acts as a moral agency that regulates behaviour. And the ego is sandwiched in-between, mediating the wants and requirements of id and superego. Growing up consists in learning how to deal with each part and finding a balance.

Newborn children are all instinct and biological impulse. They only learn to control and repress immediate wants gradually, by internalizing the demands of society imparted to them by their caregivers. The ego grows out of the id as that part of it that has been modified by external influence. It is the decision-making component of the personality that works on the basis of the 'reality principle', which contrasts with the 'pleasure principle' of the id in that it encompasses the ability to devise realistic strategies for achieving satisfaction.

Both id and ego seek pleasure and reward, but lack any moral guidelines as to how to achieve it in an acceptable way. This is where the superego comes into play. It contains the moral standards of the immediate and wider social environment. Socialization consists in internalizing these standards, a process for which Freud introduced the concept of 'identifying with'. By striving to be like people in their environment, assimilating their views, values, and ways of acting, children identify with them, the first models typically being parents and siblings. Subsequently, they transfer these properties and increasingly identify with themselves, eventually acquiring their own identity during adolescence.

However, coming of age is not the end of psychological development. Seeking other role models, such as political leaders, religious gurus, sports idols, YouTube stars, diet experts, and celebrities may continue through adulthood as a way of connecting individual with collective identity, though the propensity to adjust values and to adopt new ideals diminishes with advancing age.

In addition to values and social norms, the superego part of one's identity includes an 'ideal self', that is, an image of what you want to be. When your actions deviate from what you would expect from your ideal self—by getting drunk, violating traffic regulations, or committing a crime—your superego may interfere with your conduct and make you experience a bad conscience, a sense of guilt or shame. The two most common strategies to deal with this painful state of mind are repression (you consign your failure to the unconscious) and rationalization (you find a justification for going beyond the speed limit, evading taxes, or torturing other human beings).

When neither repression nor rationalization works and you can no longer suffer the rupture between your ideal self and your real self, you may be in need of professional help by a psychiatrist (or, if you are Catholic, a priest who absolves you of your sins 'in the name of the Father, and of the Son, and of the Holy Spirit').

A sense of crisis

Things can go wrong. Adolescents may fail to develop an integrated and well-adapted identity, and confession, absolution, rationalization, even psychological guidance may not resolve the ensuing problems. The unwelcome results include identity conflict, role confusion, anxiety, fear of having no identity, and a loss of self.

Enter Erik Erikson. It is safe to say that the Western obsession with identity would not be what it is if it wasn't for him. His work around the middle of the 20th century served as the psychological catalyst of it and today fulfils this function more than ever. Erikson was a student of Sigmund Freud's and like his teacher a psychoanalyst and anthropologist of high repute. He invented (or discovered?) the *identity crisis*. Both words, 'invent' and 'discover', do not quite accurately describe what Erikson did and why he had such a strong influence on psychology. Building on Freud's theory that conceptualized individual development as a synergy between internal drives and cultural demands, he gave a name to a phenomenon that was in the air, striking a chord that people could, indeed felt compelled to, respond to. If, as Freud had taught, personal identity derives from calibrating the individual's dependence on others with his or her needs and desires, then it stands to reason that complicated relations with others in early life can lead to an identity crisis.

Erikson developed this idea into a theory of 'ego identity' embedded in psychosocial development. He used this term to stress the priority over external social influences he gave to the ego. Yet his psychology of identity has a strong social component, which is one of the reasons why his notion of identity crisis spread so easily to other social sciences. What then is an identity crisis?

Erikson's theory of psychosocial development distinguishes eight stages of development from infancy to late adulthood, as summarized in Table 2.

Erikson's major concern was with how adolescents in interaction with their social environment form a coherent perception of self. A crisis occurs when coherence is not accomplished. Adolescence is a critical stage of identity forming, but the potential of identity crisis remains in adulthood, too, as indicated by the opposing inclinations listed under 'Conflict' in Table 2. Individuals suffering an identity crisis are insecure, do not always know where they belong, and, in extreme cases, are uncertain who or what they are. The notion 'identity crisis' presupposes, as a condition of leading a crisis-free life in harmony with yourself, a stable identity that comprises a subjective sense of personal sameness and firmness of beliefs and values. A sound personal identity consists of bodily constitution and command thereof, mental capacities, family and

Table 2. Erik Erikson's stages of personality development.

Age	Conflict	Focus
≤ 1	Trust vs mistrust	Developing trust
≤ 3	Autonomy vs shame	Self-control
≤ 6	Initiative vs guilt	Creativeness
≤ 12	Industry vs inferiority	Skills and social norms
≤ 18	Identity vs role confusion	Personality integration
≤ 30	Intimacy vs isolation	Love
Adulthood	Generativity vs stagnation	Family, career
Old age	Integrity vs despair	Existential identity (one's life)

wider social relations, and cultural heritage, all woven into one cohesive thread that persists through time without major breaks.

In the psychological sense, identity does not preclude change, but the changes that occur with progressing age do not undermine the sense of self. Identity formation is an ongoing process of adaptation to mutable environmental conditions. In their teenage years, people experience corporeal, mental, and social vicissitudes more overtly than earlier and later in life and are therefore more at risk of identity confusion. Yet identity crisis or personality breakdown can occur later in life. When your professional career takes a downturn, when your marriage comes to an end, or when you feel that you have disappointed others or have not accomplished your purpose in life, self-loathing or depression may ensue.

Identity crisis is a persuasive notion that brings together the bio-psychological source of the infant's identification with his or her caregivers with the adaptation of social norms. It is the core element of a theory connecting the individual with society by way of stressing the importance of satisfactory identifications for personality integration. A psychologically healthy person is one whose ego identity is clearly delineated and recognizable as such to self and others.

From individual to group

The term 'identity crisis' became so widely used, first in the US and then throughout the Western world, that it cannot be attributed to Erikson's perceptive and successful work alone. It must be seen also as giving expression to the *zeitgeist* of the mid-20th century. The world had gone through a horrendous war encompassing the greatest genocide in history. Millions were orphaned, uprooted, and displaced. Decolonization was in full swing, forcing the white man to reflect on his role in history and, perhaps, on his identity. At the same time, new forms of production and consumption furthered individualism and self-reliance, to the extent that many were increasingly at a loss to find their place in a society described in an influential study by David Riesman as 'The Lonely Crowd'.

Against this background, the concepts of identity and identity crisis came to be transferred from individuals to groups, small and large. Just as the individual strives for psychological security by identifying with the behaviour and values of significant persons in the environment, people who share some common features, such as ethnicity, religion, and nation, will strive to evoke a shared sense of identity.

The metaphor of a collectivity as a body—they rose as one man—facilitated looking at mass dynamics through the lens of psychological identity theory. Sociologists argue that a sane cohesive society is impossible without a collective sense of belonging to a bigger whole as a source of security, pride, and self-esteem. That is what satisfactory group identification consists of. External threats to loosely knit groups tend to reinforce group consciousness, as their members may exert more effort to enhance and protect their identity. And just as irresolvable conflicts between values, ideals, and life goals may throw the individual into an identity crisis, so it may happen with groups that confront contradicting priorities and ideals.

Nowadays, there is no limit to the kinds of subjects to which an identity crisis can be attributed: neighbourhoods, streets, markets, villages, towns, cities, countries, entire continents, military alliances, political parties, churches, companies, banks, football teams, schools, and on and on. This is not just an inflationary figure of speech, but a symptom and a manifestation of the uneasiness that many experience in the face of the rapid changes characteristic of our time: 'I no longer recognize the country/town/neighbourhood/street I grew up in.' A sense of loss of something familiar and the inability to keep up with change is seen as a deviation from the 'normal' state of affairs, an identity crisis.

A second source of the proliferation of identity crises is branding. City branding is a gold rush of consumer capitalism, and just one of many. Without an identity, you are nothing, the *you*, in the event, not being a person but a ski resort (*Vail, like nothing on earth*), a city (*Welcome to fabulous Las Vegas*), a country (*Incredible India*), a continent (*Inspiring a Great Africa*), anything that sells. When it no longer does, it must be suffering an identity crisis.

A vital part of every identity—of a person, a group, a corporation— is that it is different from other identities. It does not exist naturally but must be marked off, exhibited, enacted. This is what marketing is about, not just in the corporate world. Image, reputation, and recognizability play a similar role in enacting personal identity.

Acts of identity

In his comedy *As You Like It*, William Shakespeare has one of its characters declare: 'All the world's a stage, and all the men and women merely players'. Some three and a half centuries later, sociologist Erving Goffman published his book *The Presentation of Self in Everyday Life*, which is devoted to the question of how and following what kind of prompts 'all the men and women' act on the stage of society. People have a sense of who they are; they are self-conscious or self-confident and act accordingly. In any event, they act. Goffman's 'dramaturgical analysis' was a new approach to understanding personal identity as a role-play that is constantly under review by actors who absorb and respond to the feedback of socially relevant others.

Identity is an ensemble of features, costumes, fashion items, behaviours, speech styles, and gestures, collaboratively manufactured with others and hung on the peg of a self. Depending on the scene in which we have a part to play, we use the available tools to shape our body, bring ourselves into a suitable state of mind, and adjust our comportment. There are expectations, such as social norms and codes of conduct, we are or are not able to meet, and there are capabilities and preferences that make us enact a part more or less credibly, perhaps with a silicone implant in our lips or buttocks.

In situations such as job interviews, customer service, preaching and lecturing, and other professional encounters the performance character of our behaviour is very apparent, but we have ideas and scripts about our self in the private sphere, too. That we can 'let loose and be ourselves' is an illusion in that we cannot shed off our socialization and do not cease to exist as social beings once we close the door behind us and retreat into solitude. The cues in the private sphere will not be the same as in the public sphere, but act we must. In being aware of the theatrical character of our performance, we may call it 'second nature', not realizing that there is no 'first'; for as nature beings, humans are not viable. They are never human beings only, unconstrained by family relations, gender typing, age grading, class stratification, and ethnic pecking order.

The everyday-life drama follows different plots and directions on stage and backstage, but in both settings the actors are involved in social interaction. The stage is inhabited by other actors who perform in front of an audience whose interpretation of the scene is indispensable for the presented selves to emerge. In this way, the individual actors forge their self-identities within the framework of traditions and institutional requirements, which by acting they help to reinforce or transform. Backstage they are no longer Romeo and Juliet, Peer Gynt or Mother Courage; instead, they are professional actors who as such have a standing in society, living in a certain world, interacting with others of their kind and of other walks of life. Their social reality differs from that of office clerks and factory workers as much as from that of medieval ladies in waiting and knights.

Everybody always acts; which means that personal identity, rather than being given, is created in the interaction of self with others. Everyone cannot participate in every scene or enact every role that requires specific talents and acquired competencies. And, to stay with the metaphor, as an actor you may represent a respectable traditional art in one society, the demimonde in another, and the creative class in a third.

Just as with professional acting, so with other professions and social roles. Norms and expectations attached to them may differ markedly from one socio-cultural system to another. People who move between two systems, therefore, feel that to present *their* self in everyday life they have to act differently, adjusting to the stage directions of the place where the scene is set. Those who are able to do so easily have been said to switch between two identities,

97

while those who are not may feel, and be perceived as, out of place in one of the settings or in both.

Culture and personal identity

Psychologists would typically diagnose a person who displays a fragmented identity as abnormal. Such a state, however, is not the same as the ability to move from one stage to another and to perform with similar effects in front of different audiences by acting differently. This is not necessarily pathological, but can be evidence of bicultural competence. A simple example is the tactful tourist who knows to cover her shoulders in St Peter's Basilica in Rome and her head in the Jama Masjid in New Delhi. It is easy to avoid being offensive, but it takes cultural knowledge to blend in and present the person you want to be in different settings.

This has been overlooked for a long time, since psychological theories of personal identity were predicated on universalist assumptions, although they were developed in Western societies for Western people. Yet, Freud's concept of the superego and similar concepts derived thereof that relate social influence to psychic development inevitably raises the question of socio-cultural components of individual identity.

Research suggests, for instance, that Japanese American women—the very same individuals—act more assertively in the US than in Japan. This is in keeping with stereotypes and generalizations about the position of women in both societies. People behave in different ways with different people without thereby betraying their 'true self' or plunging into an identity crisis.

Since few psychologists subscribe to unmodulated genetic determinism of individual development, culture occupies a place in personal identity theory. You are born as a biological being, but what it means to be a white woman or a black man or a 'bastard' you only learn in a society that calls one that. The variables that go into identity formation are not the same everywhere.

The indigenization of psychology outside the Western world led to the discovery of personality traits and to the development of analytic concepts that Western individualism de-emphasizes or ignores. *Kapwa* or 'shared inner self' is such a concept that Filipino psychologists proposed as a core value of the Filipino psyche. It integrates elements of Confucian ethics, mutual trust, a sense of being one with others, and the ability to adapt and surrender one's identity in favour of conformity.

The Japanese notion of *amae* or 'passive love' is another example of an analytic concept strongly linked to a non-Western culture. It expresses the desire unconditionally to be loved and being cared for by a trusted other. Both *kapwa* and *amae* have invited criticism and debate in their national contexts and beyond. The importance of these concepts is not that they have conclusively pinpointed personality traits so far overlooked, but to call attention to the fact that if identity formation involves acts of identifying with, the range of values, mores, and models offered to the individual to this end has to be taken into account. This is a project of merging individual psychology with cultural psychology by way of acknowledging the possibility of a Eurocentric bias in established theories of personal identity formation, without falling into the trap of unqualified cultural relativism.

Adjusting to how things are done in one's environment is part and parcel of individual identity formation. This is nowhere more obvious than in language (which is both nature and culture).

Conclusions

Rather than a fixed state, personal identity is an ongoing project. The individual forms his or her identity by *identifying with* someone or something. Individuals who are unable to reconcile competing personal and social demands may suffer an identity crisis, an experience once associated with adolescence, which, however, in recent decades has been linked to mental troubles in adult life stages, too. Personal identity is something we are, something we have, and something we act. We perform acts of identity following culture-specific stage directions that leave room for individual expressivity.

Chapter 9

'They don't speak our language': identity in linguistics

Your smartphone vibrates. You listen. 'Hello, this—' and already you know who is calling. A syllable or two may be enough to identify the speaker.

On 27 September 2014, Indian Prime Minister Narendra Modi addressed the UN General Assembly, in Hindi. This was more important than what he had to say. He was the first Indian prime minister to do so, rather than speak English.

These two events represent the large bandwidth of the relationship between language and identity. Language is so exclusive that it distinguishes every speaker from all others, and so inclusive that it binds 490 million speakers of Hindi together to form a community. This double function makes language the paradigm of an identity marker.

The mother tongue

'Mother tongue' is a powerful metaphor. What is closer to ourselves, what is more important for our humanity, physically and mentally, what links us more firmly with our community than our mother? The image of the mother tongue conveys security and at the same time the ability to understand others and act together. It distinguishes us from barbarians, as the

Greeks in antiquity called all non-Greek-speaking peoples. The image also insinuates naturalness, an innate faculty we are born with. Like our mother, our mother tongue is unique. It is close to our heart and has qualities unlike any other—or so the prevalent European language ideology suggests.

What 'mother tongue' actually means is open to interpretation. To begin with, many people cannot answer the question of what their mother tongue is in the singular. It is difficult to put a hard figure on it, but about half the world population grow up with two or more languages. Next, if your mother tongue is English, what exactly does that mean? East Anglian English, Cockney, Anglo-Cornish, Bengali English, Gulf Southern, African American Vernacular English, Ottawa Valley English, Inupiaq English? Speakers of these and scores of other varieties may not easily understand each other, yet they can all rightly claim to be native speakers of English. This is because 'native speaker' and 'mother tongue' are ill-defined terms that have an emotional content but no clear meaning. Professional linguists do not use these terms without defining them or eschew them altogether.

Every normal child is born with the capacity to acquire language, any one of the 7,000 or so languages spoken on the planet. Counting languages is a vain endeavour. The question where language A ends and language B begins has no non-arbitrary answer. Linguists therefore use the term 'named languages', thus highlighting the difficulty of separating languages one from another and establishing their identity. However, regardless of what linguists think, politically induced language boundaries may acquire a social reality precisely because of the potential of minor linguistic differences to demarcate boundaries.

The multitude of human idioms directs our attention to the important difference between *language* and *languages*, the former being a natural, humanity-defining capacity, while the latter are cultural artefacts. We can activate the general capacity of language only by acquiring a particular language. The bio-social process enabling us to do that remains unconscious, but thanks to the nature–culture mix that is peculiar to every language, languages can so easily be commissioned for identity purposes.

Languages are artefacts in the sense that every single word of every single language has been coined, or borrowed from another, by someone (rather than having grown like flowers in the field or whispered in our ears by the wind). They do not seem artificial like Esperanto; but in the end, many (especially written) languages are just as artificial, if we accept that to boldly split infinitives and other transgressions are sinful. Many languages are consciously cultivated as the medium to convey our thoughts, valuable receptacles of tradition, links that connect our offspring to our forebears, and as symbols of our identity. However, we find manifestations of linguistic identity on many different levels that are beyond the control of professional guardians of language.

Dimensions of linguistic identity

Modi's speech at the UN was an act of identity: Here speaks the prime minister of a Hindu nation, rather than an heir to the British Raj. At the level of nation states, languages serve the symbolic function of identity manifestation, like flags and other emblems of nationhood. Throughout the 19th and 20th centuries, linguistic nationalism inspired many a political conflict, as the consolidation of nation states was accompanied by a division between national languages and other languages. That the government in Islamabad made Urdu Pakistan's national language was a key factor triggering the secession of the eastern part of the country, where nobody spoke Urdu. On 21 February, Bangladesh still commemorates the Bengali language movement as 'Martyr's Day'. Scripts and writing systems are particularly popular symbols of national identity, as illustrated by Qazaqstan's recent decision to replace the heavily Russian-tinged Cyrillic attire of its language with what its leaders hope will be a more independent Roman outfit. If you use simplified rather than traditional Chinese characters in Hong Kong, you are a friend of Beijing.

Next, on the subnational level *dialects* manifest linguistic identity. Dialectologists have developed sophisticated methods to describe the characteristic variables and minute differences of regional speech objectively in terms of accent patterns, vocabulary, grammar, etc. Subjectively, these differences are emotionally charged for speakers of the varieties in question and for others. While for its speakers a dialect may evoke familiarity, closeness, and warmth, it may be an object of disgust and derision for others.

Evaluations of this sort betray the social dimension of language variation. Some dialects are more prestigious than others, not because of their inherent qualities, but because their speakers are more powerful, wealthy, and well thought of. Geographically, prestige grading often coincides with urban–rural and capital–provinces contrasts. *Standard* English/French/German/ Spanish etc. is the language of power and, therefore, highly regarded.

Language variation is multi-layered, local dialects being just one dimension. All other features of social and personal identity discussed in previous chapters have a linguistic manifestation, too. *Sociolects* correlating with class have been the object of study in industrialized countries where income, kind of work, level of education, and lifestyle have overlaid urban–rural divisions.

The observation in 1960s Britain that working-class speech was a predictor of lower academic achievement prompted much research by educationalists and sociolinguists, as well as a public debate about how to deal with this problem. Should working-class pupils learn middle-class speech, or should schools learn to cope with working-class speech? Compensation for deficit, or recognition of diversity?

In the 1980s, a similar discussion arose about African American Vernacular English (AAVE) or Black English in the United States, where race is a more prominent factor of social division than class. Those who regarded AAVE as a sign of low scholastic aptitude were pitted against those who saw in 'spoken Soul'—to use a phrase coined by Stanford linguist John Rickford—a legitimate language tradition meriting preservation for the sake of identity. For a while, the latter promoted *Ebonics* as a positive label for a stigmatized variety, some even with the intention of declaring linguistic independence from English. However, most African Americans did not accept this as a viable strategy to improve their position in US society.

Investigating and describing the subtleties of AAVE was the starting signal for research on a great number of *ethnolects*, that is, varieties of a majority language associated with immigrant groups, such as Chicano English in California, Moroccan Dutch in Rotterdam, or Turkish German in Berlin. At the same time, metropolitan centres like New York City, London, Manchester, Amsterdam, Brussels, and Melbourne saw dozens if not hundreds of immigrant communities assert their identity by promoting their heritage (or community) language.

Yet another dimension of the language variation complex is gender. *Genderlects* differ one from another, and the differences between them vary in intensity and kind across languages, carrying different socio-cultural meanings. Gendered language use involves pitch, word selection, hedging, and degrees of directness, among others. The feminist agenda to uncover the connection between gender stereotypes, language, and sexism paved the way for a better understanding of the social functions of speech styles. Meanwhile the duet of male and female voices has been expanded to include the registers of LGBTQ speakers, summarily referred to as 'Lavender language'.

Because, along with other biological features, the vocal apparatus of women and men is different, it is widely believed that gendered ways of speaking are natural. However, stylistic distinctions, even pitch, which is most likely to reflect physical conditions, are interlaced with social stereotypes whereby males and females are assigned specific roles. It can be difficult, therefore, to separate natural from cultural aspects of linguistic gender identity.

Pitch is one of the features of speech that change with age, like word choice. Language is a tool we permanently adjust to our communication needs and thus change; but we also retain certain features marking it out as characteristic of our generation. Younger and older stages of life have their own in-group codes—methinks.

Finally, we each have our own voice quality, style, and mannerisms, which constitute an *idiolect* distinct from all others. The scientific study of speech recognition has matured to a level reliable enough for forensic purposes, and automatic speaker recognition software is widely employed for gatekeeping applications. A voice, then, is to the ear what handwriting is to the eye.

In sum, your way of speaking gives you away. After listening to a recording of your voice for a while, a trained linguist may come to the conclusion that you are a white middle-aged college-educated lesbian solicitor who grew up in Lancashire and whose father was/is probably Canadian. You may or may not be aware of the features the linguist has recognized, emphasizing one or some of them deliberately by way of identifying with a group and 'presenting yourself in everyday life'.

The parameters of linguistic identity can be ordered in the following hierarchy:

National language
Dialect
Sociolect
Ethnolect
Heritage/community language
Genderlect
Age-specific code
Idiolect

Linguism and other isms

Linguists believe that any language is as good as any other, all
languages being a manifestation of the human faculty of language.
Many non-linguists do not share this belief, holding that Sanskrit
is the eternal language, perfect and unchanging; that Italian is
the language of romance; that English is cool; that certain accents
are inferior to others; that some ways of speaking are beautiful
and others ugly. Perceptual dialectology is the scientific study of
attitudes of this sort, which invariably lead to discrimination of
one kind or another. It is easier to say, 'What a dreadful dialect!'
than 'I hate these guys'.

Praise and scorn of language varieties testify to the important
role language plays for group identification. The defacing of the
Irish part of bilingual English and Irish road signs in Ulster is a
hate crime directed against a bilingual language policy and a
conciliatory attitude towards neighbouring Ireland.

Dual-language road signs are a favourite target of linguistic
chauvinists. They are in plain view, and no one has any doubt that
the vandalized signpost is just a stand-in for the speakers of the
wiped-out language.

And so it is with other dimensions of linguistic identity. Mimicking
a dialect, ethnolect, sociolect or genderlect is an effective
strategy to mock someone. A key element of impersonating

politicians or other prominent people is imitating their way of speaking, a skill that stand-up comedians exaggerate to humorous effect. Acting generally involves employing speech varieties suitable to the embodied character.

Speech caricature can be denigrating and upsetting precisely because it touches the victim's personality. For the same reason, telling someone that they are talking like 'a fag', 'an old whore', or 'a white boy' is considered offensive rather than a matter-of-fact description, regardless of how true it may be. Taking issue with language in one of its forms that are associated with groups or individuals may be a masked attack on that group or individual grounded upon xenophobia, sexism, or nationalism.

Every language variety from national language to idiolect can be enlisted for identity manifestation and, accordingly, be venerated or despised, praised or denigrated. For every kind of linguistic identity, an ism exists that puts it down.

The linguistic identity of individuals

Imitating another speaker is funny for two reasons. It requires the manipulation of behavioural features that usually remain unconscious, and it reminds us of the fact that every person's speech is unique. That extortionists made telephone calls with a pencil between the teeth is lore long past. Nowadays voice-changing software is routinely employed, for instance, to protect the identity of interviewees who fear for their safety. However, the antidote for unmasking modulated voices also exists. Voice biometrics is a growth industry.

Voice identification by spectrographic analysis is a long-established method of forensic linguistics. With big data, it has achieved a new quality. Audio files of speech samples are transformed into visual data called voiceprints or spectrograms (Figure 12). This involves the measurement of the physical

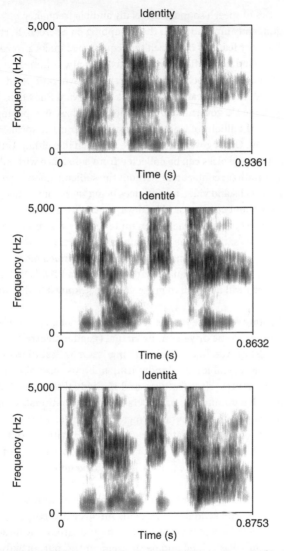

12. Voiceprints of the words *identity*, *identité* (French), and *identità* (Italian), pronounced by the author.

properties of speech sounds, especially audible frequency, duration, and amplitude, and their mapping on a screen. Further identificatory features of speech that combine to make a voice unique include the following: prosody, velocity, volume, dialect/sociolect, speech defect (e.g. lisp), idiosyncratic word choice and grammatical constructions. As Edward Snowden revealed, the US government maintains a database comprising hundreds of millions of voices prepared for automatic speaker recognition. Other governments have not been idle either. Unlike DNA samples, voices can be collected from a distance without direct or indirect contact and without the subject's knowledge, telephone calls and video conferences being there for the taking, with or without consent or official warrant. With a recording of a person's voice, you can track them quite reliably wherever they have a conversation. One's voice, and more generally one's idiolect, is a personal identity marker, which is much more difficult to change than a name, an address, or a PIN. ('OK Google' voice search will help you to make your voice known to the world.)

Handwriting is likewise very hard to imitate, although pen*man*ship seems bound to be driven out by virtual (gender-neutral) keyboardship. Yet, like speech, writing is a manifestation of identity on several levels. Handwriting analysis recognizes national features, class features, and individual features that distinguish communities of writers. A writer's national, social, and educational background permeates his or her writing, independent of medial materialization as handwriting, print, or screen. Spelling and punctuation may help to identify/verify the writer of a blackmail letter, last will, or suicide note.

Other methods of author identification include historical lexicography and stylometry. Drawing on large text corpora, historical lexicography can say with a high degree of accuracy when a word was coined and became current. A purportedly 18th-century text that includes 20th-century words is thus suspicious. Stylometry looks for characteristic stylistic patterns, using statistics, for example, about the total size of a writer's lexicon and the frequency of occurrence of types of words and collocations. Sophisticated computer programs can process huge amounts of text to uncover patterns the unaided reader cannot easily recognize.

These quantitative methods have opened up new approaches to authorship attribution of both historical and contemporary literary works. For forensic and law enforcement purposes they are also increasingly applied to online texts.

Individual parameters of language variation allow speakers and writers to exhibit their identity and at the same time make it difficult to escape from it.

The identity of languages

In view of the many identificatory features of language distinguishing groups and individuals, it is perhaps not surprising that people project their ideas of and needs for identity and group membership onto the medium that facilitates participation: their primary language. They reify their language, conceiving of it as a thing, or rather a living organism with its own identity. As soon as a language becomes part of formal education or is dominated by another such language, its speakers tend to essentialize it as 'our soul', 'our cultural fingerprint', 'the cornerstone of our national pride', 'a mirror of the nation', 'the preserve of our cultural memory', etc. Praise of one's own language is as common as the idea that it is unique and, therefore, worth defending against others and protecting from decay.

More than 150 language academies and other regulatory agencies throughout the world watch over the development of languages, following the examples of the Italian *Accademia della Crusca* (founded 1583) and the French *Académie française* (founded 1635). Typically, these institutions promote the standardization of the language in question, compiling dictionaries and reference grammars as well as teaching materials for disseminating it. They all operate on the somewhat contradictory assumption that their language has a natural immutable identity that must be controlled. Conceptually this is possible for a similar reason that humans and other living creatures are thought to have an identity. They change perpetually, yet they persist through time.

Direct identification of a language with a people or ethnic group implies a commitment to its survival, which is equated with the survival of the group. This attitude lies behind the fact that political nationalism often breeds linguistic nationalism. Like the former, the latter finds expression in xenophobia, which in the case of language manifests itself as purism. Much as racists portray immigrants as undermining the integrity of 'our people', purists fight the contamination of 'our language' by loanwords. The fact that all languages have always interacted with others and there is, accordingly, no pure language on earth does not concern them. Instead of the historically attested interconnectedness, they emphasize borders. Ethnic cleansing has its linguistic counterpart in lexical purification, sequestering or proscribing foreign elements.

The analogy between race and language carries a long way in as much as, like in the case of race, the 'pure language' is a scientifically untenable, but still socially powerful idea, which is to show that languages cannot be reduced to the instrumental function of content communication. The notion that they have an identity rooted in, and uniquely suited to expressing, the inner self of the people is deeply ingrained and always ready to serve symbolic purposes of identity politics.

Conclusions

For individuals and groups, language has instrumental and symbolic functions, which can be in conflict with each other.

The instrumental function of communication stands for inclusion, the symbolic function of identity manifestation, for exclusion. Language serves identity manifestation with regard to nation, region, social class, ethnicity (race), gender, and age. The respective linguistic differences can be highlighted or downplayed. Yet, on the level of individual expression in both speech and writing, language has biometric qualities allowing for highly reliable speaker identification.

Chapter 10
Who is behind the mask?
Identity in literature

The mask

The actors in classical Greek tragedy all wore masks on stage, separating themselves from the spectators more than the stage itself could. The mask is a sign not to kill the messenger and at the same time elevates the theatre stage to a platform of ritual performance 'out of this world'. Artistes of the *Commedia dell'arte* in Renaissance Italy revived the classical tradition using masks to enact stereotyped roles.

The Chinese opera and Japanese Noh are also highly ceremonialized theatres that make use of masks bearing symbolic meaning. They signify the characters' age, gender, social status, and personality, which may not concur with the actors' own properties. These masks stylize and codify emotions and character traits, a dramatic technique that also inspired modern playwrights such as W. B. Yeats, Eugene O'Neill, and Bertolt Brecht.

Italian dramatist Luigi Pirandello saw in masks a theatrical convention most appropriate for modern times where the sense of individual singleness is under constant threat, a point he put on stage in his play *Six Characters in Search of an Author*. In it, six actors who are about to rehearse for a play by Pirandello are unexpectedly interrupted by six characters who inform them that they are in search of an author. Pirandello thus shows how reality and illusion are interconnected. Reflecting on the function of the mask in a similar spirit, French dramatist and critic André Gide asked, 'Where is the mask?—In the audience, or on the stage? In the theatre, or in life?'

The mask reminds the audience and the actor that he or she is not the person whose actions are being performed. Costume and makeup fulfil similar functions, and minimalist theatre does without any of these props, as do children. They act to play and play to learn, and in Venice and Rio de Janeiro their parents once a year join them, taking Carnival as licence to put on a mask and become things they are not.

The mask, then, symbolizes the difference between a fictitious identity and a real identity, or perhaps better, between what passes as the difference between fiction and reality. There is an actor behind the mask who represents someone else, which, however, he could not do if he were someone else. The audience may be gripped by the story that unfolds onstage, but they applaud the actress for her performance. This is the backdrop of many literary works of all genres in which questions of identity turn up ubiquitously.

Themes

In literature, we can find all the aspects and dimensions of identity discussed in the previous chapters: identity through time, the mind–body problem, the identity of words and things, gender boundaries, identity crisis, divided loyalty, mistaken identity, split identity, and the demands of modernity for individuals to have a national, social, and gender identity. Some conspicuous and representative examples illustrate.

Recognition and persistence through time

When after twenty years Odysseus returned to his home in Ithaca, he was mistaken for an old beggar. Until by shooting with his mighty bow the rowdy suitors of his wife he revealed his true identity, only his wet nurse Eurykleia, washing his feet, recognized him from an immutable identity mark, a scar on his leg. This story from *The Odyssey* (verse 467) must be one of the first in world literature on recognition and persistence of identity through time. To change while staying the same and being recognized as such by others is an eternal theme that occupied ancient Greek philosophers and still occupies their successors today.

Mistaken identity

The topos of mistaken identity likewise shows up in the earliest dramas. Plautus, a Roman playwright of the 2nd century BCE, was a master of the theme. For instance, in his comedy *Menaechmi* he composes a tale of confusion and deception involving twin brothers who were separated at a young age and through a sequence of coincidences and a benevolent fate happily reunited as grown-up men.

Plautus became something of a patron saint of comedy, his plays a source of inspiration for many writers. Like *Menaechmi*, William Shakespeare's *Comedy of Errors* (1594, Figure 13) deals with twin brothers caught up in multiple situations of mix-up about borrowed money, servants, and the wife of one of the brothers. To boot Shakespeare supplements the brothers with a pair of servants who are also twins. The concept of mistaken identity where twins unwittingly or deliberately fool other characters is at the heart of the plot, accounting for a succession of humorous situations.

Twins who get misidentified also play a role in other of Shakespeare's dramas, in *Twelfth Night*, for instance, where the protagonist twins

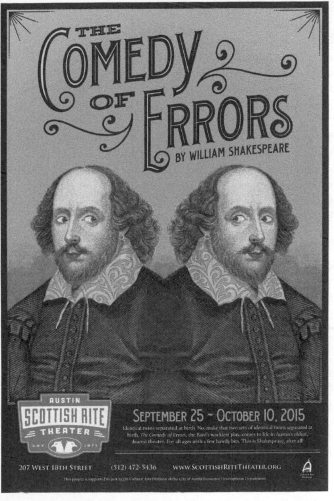

13. William Shakespeare, *The Comedy of Errors*, poster by Scottish Rite Theater, 2015.

are brother and sister, extending identity confusion to gender. The sister disguises herself as a man introducing a motif that Carlo Goldoni picked up in *The Servant of Two Masters* (1746). Here Truffaldino causes much disorder, playing a double role as servant of two masters to augment his income, while Beatrice slips into her brother Federigo's identity to make the story of promised and cancelled marriages even more perplexing.

These plays deal with funny aspects of mistaken identity, creating scenes in which characters with a certain intent conceal their identities or are mistaken by chance. The course of events, these being comedies, sometimes lands them in unexpected troubles, but they do not lose control of their true identity. However, there is no dearth of dramas devoted to the more sinister facets of self-identity.

Split identity

> You are aware of only one unrest;
> Oh, never learn to know the other!
> Two souls, alas, are dwelling in my breast,
> And one is striving to forsake its brother.

These dark lines encapsulate a major theme of Johann Wolfgang Goethe's drama *Faust* (1808). Its protagonist, an alchemist by the name of Johann Georg Faust, in an attempt to overcome the limits of human understanding, concludes a pact with Mephistopheles, forsaking his soul for boundless knowledge. In the end, Faust is no match for the devil, and his quest for salvation in the absence of a soul to be salvaged ends in disaster. Faust's name is appropriately ambiguous. In German, *Faust* ('fist') stands for wrath and brute force; in Latin, however, *faustus* means 'happy'. Pursuing happiness with brute force is destined to fail. Faust makes us see that thirst for knowledge and humility vis-à-vis the infinite universe cannot be happily separated, that renouncing one's soul is no method of forcing one's luck.

Faust's torn self is a literary archetype that inspired many dramatists, poets, and composers to adapt various elements of the story in their own interpretations. The discordant sides of the protagonist's identity, swayed between good and evil, between noble goals and dubious means, between hubris and trust in God, unite them all.

With his novella *The Wonderful History of Peter Schlemihl* (1814), Adelbert von Chamisso created the disquieting tale of a man who acquires a new identity as Count Peter by parting with his shadow in exchange for bottomless wealth. Recounted in a realistic manner, the story's only inexplicable element is Peter's detached shadow. Since a world without shadows is not physically possible, Peter, so as not to attract too much attention, is forced to live in the dark, and the reader is left to wonder whether and how one's shadow could be part of one's identity.

Doppelgänger

The 19th century saw the publication of a long list of doppelgänger narratives. In E. T. A. Hoffmann's 1816 short story 'The Sandman' one of the characters tries to represent an automaton as a living person. Edgar Allan Poe's 'William Wilson' (1839) is about a man's fight with his identically named replica. Feodor Dostoevsky's *The Double* (1846) tells the story of Yakov Petrovich Golyadkin's struggle with himself, as he goes mad. And Guy de Maupassant's 'The Terror' (1883) is about a nameless man who is afraid of himself.

Robert Louis Stevenson's novella *The Strange Case of Dr Jekyll and Mr Hyde* (1886) became the literary exemplar of the clash of a man with himself. Hyde is Jekyll's evil self whom he, Jekyll, tries to control by means of a potion, but in the course of time, Hyde is threatening to win the upper hand. After protracted efforts to regain control, self-destruction is Jekyll's only way out.

Oscar Wilde developed the shadow identity theme in *The Picture of Dorian Gray* (1890), in which shameless and narcissistic Dorian is confronted with his immoral self in the form of a picture that grows older and uglier with every evil act he commits.

The doppelgänger motif entails the logical inconsistency of encountering oneself as another and (failing to) unite 'I' and 'not-I' into one identity. Its literary representation in the works just mentioned has been read as foreshadowing the idea of identity crisis that so preoccupied 20th-century psychology. They have invited a wealth of psychological and psychosocial interpretations, including Sigmund Freud's examination of the 'uncanny' based on his psychoanalytic reading of Hoffmann's 'The Sandman'.

Body and mind

Another logical inconsistency is to do with the mind–body problem. As Gregor Samsa wakes up in the morning, he finds himself transformed into a giant insect. Thus begins Franz Kafka's story 'The Metamorphosis' (1915). Gregor hears raindrops hitting against the window. The world seems rather normal, except for the enigmatic detail of Gregor's body swap. But Gregor is Gregor, and as the story unfolds, nothing suggests that it could be otherwise, notably Gregor himself continues to believe that he is himself, a different body, but the same mind.

Thomas Mann's 1940 novella *The Transposed Heads: A Legend from India* calls into question the mind over matter notion that 'The Metamorphosis' suggests, and indeed the mind/body dualism of the Western tradition. There are two friends, an athlete and an intellectual, who love the same woman. Only one can marry her; the other one decides to get out of the way, cutting off his own head. His distraught friend follows his example, leaving the woman without friend or husband. With the help of a goddess, the friends are revived, but heads and bodies are switched in the process.

The clever head on the strong body looks like the ideal spouse, but this turns out to be a delusion. Both men are misfits; as time goes by, personalities change and in the end all three of them perish in desperation. In hindsight, this peculiar tale seems eerily prescient of current discussions of a whole body transplant, also called a brain transplant, which focus not only on what is technically possible, but also on the ethical implications of such an operation and the question of what makes an integrated self. The morale of Mann's story affirms the psychosomatic unity of our identity as human beings.

Lost in modernity

For a person to be whole and at ease with him or herself, it is not just body and mind that have to be in harmony, but also the individual and the social self. The difficulties of achieving this are a leitmotif of 20th century literature.

Robert Musil's *The Man without Qualities* (1930) is set in Vienna as the curtain falls on the Habsburg monarchy, where the protagonist struggles to adjust to modernity, mentally, politically, and culturally. Albert Camus's *The Stranger* (1942), set in French Algeria, revolves around the role of death for finding one's identity. The man without properties, Ulrich, has no last name, while the stranger, Meursault, has no first name. Giving them a full name would be tantamount to acknowledging that they have what they don't have, a well-defined identity.

Both Ulrich and Meursault are dispassionate and rather detached from the world around them. Their stories are incomparable as regards plot, length, and philosophical embedding. What allows them to be put next to each other is their critical stance vis-à-vis modern ideas of subjectivity and identity, especially in terms of nationality, race, culture, social class, and gender. Meursault is a stranger to society who, in view of the insignificance of human affairs in the universe, is ready to leave the world without regret. There is no destiny. Ulrich's story confirms just that. It takes place in a world where 'sharp borderlines everywhere became blurred' and ends without an end, the search for identity incomplete.

A few years later, in 1948, Irish writer Samuel Beckett published his play *En attendant Godot* (the English translation of the original French is *Waiting for Godot*, 1953) about an absent figure. In it two tramps hang around waiting for one Godot who never comes. When Beckett was asked who or what Godot was, he tersely replied, 'if I knew, I would have said so in the play'. In the course of the play, various characteristics of Godot are mentioned without making his identity any less enigmatic. The question 'Who is Godot?' remains unanswered.

Yukio Mishima's 1949 novel *Confessions of a Mask* grapples with another ill-fated search for identity. The main protagonist, Kochan, is a young homosexual who grew up in Japan's era of right-wing ultra-nationalism. Confronted with intersecting social and cultural norms that he cannot reconcile with his own inclinations, he tries to fabricate an identity mask in order to fit in.

In our days, Viet Thanh Nguyen's *The Sympathizer* (2015) is an illustrative literary treatment of identity problems. The novel features a biracial double-agent who ponders the inner conflicts of an exiled Vietnamese stranded in post-Vietnam War California not being able to live his own identity in the sense the term is used in an identity-obsessed society.

And then there is *Cards of Identity*, Nigel Dennis's 1955 sardonic tale about the 'Identity Club'. Its designated new president has this to say about it:

> the way of *our* club is surely the best. We actually do live in isolation from the world—which is to say that we live in exactly the same way as all other clubs except that we do so more comfortably and don't

have to pretend that we have open minds. Our beloved theory, the only true one in the world, is the only one we want to hear about. Identity is the answer to everything.

This visionary novel anticipated the present preoccupation with identity, satirizing it but also taking it seriously and exploring its nature as a social phenomenon.

The above enumeration is not an attempt to do justice to the works cited. It just singles out some aspects that are relevant to the topic at hand to offer a glimpse, however superficial, at how polyphonic and rich an echo of the identity problematique resonates in fictional literature past and present.

In addition to informing the contents of works of fiction, identity is important in two other ways in literature that deserve to be mentioned.

Style and identity

Writing fiction involves creating identifiable characters. Many authors elaborately equip their protagonists with distinctive features that make them come alive with their own voice. In drama, this is part of the script that tells the actors how to speak their lines. In prose, authors employ stylistic techniques like the ones forensic linguistics analyses, as discussed in Chapter 9.

Some characters use certain words and expressions, some always speak in carefully crafted roundabout sentences, and some use interjections, never finishing a sentence. Since real-life speech cannot be reproduced in writing- -for example, we hear but do not see the difference between a female and a male voice—writers use symbolic techniques that evoke features of speech. Non-standard spelling, such as, 'it woz noffink' for 'it was nothing', 'wanna' for 'want to', or 'enry iggins' for 'Henry Higgins' insinuate certain characteristics, including ethnic, social, regional, and gender identity markers. What is known as 'eye dialect' is a stylistic device to portray a character's local or educational background. Skilful writers also know how to denote jargon and childlike speech. Combining both in his novel *Zazie in the Metro*, Raymond Queneau presents his foul-mouthed ten-year-old heroine by letting her say precociously, 'gzactement' for 'exactement' (exactly), 'chsuis' for 'je suis' (I am), 'a rvois' for 'au revoir' (goodbye), etc. In the event, the unconventional spelling does not systematically correspond to features of pronunciation, but rather visually characterizes Zazie in a humorous manner.

Representing foreign accents in writing is also possible, but more difficult and sometimes problematic, as readers may be unfamiliar with the targeted accent, and the author's way of representing it may be based upon and reinforce stereotypes.

What's in a name?

A large vocabulary and a broad repertoire of registers are the tools of the art of writing. By using stylistic devices to afford their characters a recognizable identity, and by composing poetry and prose in their own distinct manner, writers simultaneously establish their own identity as poets, novelists, and playwrights making a name for themselves. For writers, having a name is important. For recognition you must be recognizable. To quote an example that Bertrand Russell introduced in the identity literature of logic, 'George IV wondered whether Scott is the author of *Waverley*'. This sentence has puzzled logicians because 'Scott' refers to Scott and so does 'the author of *Waverley*'. Both expressions should therefore be considered identical, but George IV surely did not wonder whether Scott is Scott.

Writers make a name for themselves by cultivating a distinctive style. Critics applaud or censure them for their formal dexterity or clumsiness with words. They have criteria for distinguishing a great variety of literary styles, trying to put quality judgements on an objective footing. They also rely on such criteria to identify an author, for style characterizes both the written work and the writer. Moreover, there are writers who, while making a name for themselves, do not use their own. Walter Scott *was* the author of *Waverley*, but the author of *The Imaginary Invalid* was Jean-Baptiste Poquelin, rather than Molière, the name on the cover (appropriately so called).

Stylistics has long been a method philologists applied to establish the authorship of documents of unknown origin, including literary works published anonymously or under a pen name. For instance, the authentication of 'lost' Shakespeare plays used to be a cottage industry for philologists. The availability of electronic corpora and statistics software has turned it into an auspicious field of literary studies that goes far beyond traditional text analysis unaided by computers. Equipped with these tools, students of stylometry profess to have unmasked the Italian bestseller novelist who goes by the name Elena Ferrante. While their claim has not been confirmed or denied, it is evident that the new methods have made it easier and more reliable to identify an author.

His or her style becomes part of a writer's identity. Without overstretching the analogy, an author's stylistic profile can be likened to a fingerprint or a voiceprint. While these distinctive features identify an individual, they hardly constitute that individual's identity in its full depth and breadth. In addition to writing in a distinct, recognizable style, writers also have an identity as a private person and as a persona that corresponds more or less closely to their mask, that is, the projected identity of the author of *XYZ*. On occasion, writers ask themselves which one is their real self.

An intriguing example is a short story by Argentine writer Jorge Luis Borges, entitled 'Borges and I'. In the story, there are two characters. One is called 'Borges', and the other is the first person narrator 'I'. The story recounts how *I* has various relationships with *Borges*. For instance, *I* knows of *Borges* from a list of names of professors. *I* acknowledges *Borges* as a writer, but says that he can go on living, while *Borges* dedicates himself to writing. *I* also mentions that he is destined to perish, but some parts of *I* will perhaps survive in *Borges*. While these apparent contradictions are perplexing enough by themselves, we eventually also have to ask, where in all this is the fictional author of the short story whose name happens to be 'Borges'?

Russell (who, incidentally, was awarded the Nobel Prize in Literature) resolved the problem of the identity/non-identity of 'Scott' and 'author of *Waverley*' for logicians. His theory in 'On Denoting' spirited it away by reducing it to an ambiguity of *de dicto* (about what is said) and *de re* (about the thing). Borges, by contrast, rather than resolving the 'I' vs 'Borges' ambiguity leaves normal people wondering about it and the peculiar relationship between reality, fiction, names, and identity, concluding the short story thus: 'I do not know which of us has written this page.'

Conclusions

In literature we can find an echo of all of the identity problems that have occupied and continue to occupy the general public and scholarship. In addition to substantial questions of identity, the art of literature is also concerned with identity in two formal ways. Style expresses the identity of fictitious characters as well as of writers. Finally, by creating fictitious worlds that are and are not part of our world, literature constructs identity puzzles in its own right.

Conclusion: the identity of identity

What can be more identical than identity? 'Identity', the word, suggests immutability, self-sameness, permanency; while in fact it does what other words also do, it changes its meaning—in our day and age, so rapidly that it is hard to keep track.

Seven-year-old Shibuya Mirai caused a stir when, in November 2017, he received his official identity document, complete with photograph and date of birth, sealed and signed by Mayor Ken Hasebe of Shibuya ward in Tokyo. Shibuya Mirai is an artificial intelligence (AI) bot (his names means 'Shibuya's future'). At around the same time and to the surprise of many, Sophia was granted citizenship in Saudi Arabia. The disbelief was not because she is a non-Muslim woman or a foreigner. Like little Mirai, Sophia is a machine and an AI system. If another identical robot were created, it wouldn't have a separate identity, or would it?

Approaching the issue from another direction, Chinese scientists have cloned two identical long-tailed macaques, the first genuine doppelgänger primates to walk the planet. This is much closer to home than Frankenstein ever came. What shall we make of their identity/identities?

The 20th century has seen constant endeavours to give clear classifications and identities to people now tellingly referred to as 'trans'. Yet, the lines separating transvestites, transgenders, and others defying binary categories have become increasingly blurred rather than more distinct.

The same can be said about dividing lines between racial, ethnic, and linguistic identities. The word 'identity' as used in identity politics is the most blatant example confirming Humpty Dumpty's oft-quoted assertion that a word 'means just what I choose it to mean'.

On the individual level, identities have become a matter of negotiating and, as the need to do so arises, renegotiating your place, your purpose, and your presentation in everyday life. On the collective level, identities are fuzzy sets rather than clearly delineated groups. What is a European, a Bosnian, a Catalan, a woman, a Muslim, a homosexual, a dead person? Notwithstanding the impossibility of answering these questions categorically, the historical contingency of identity is widely ignored when it comes to defending that which is 'genuinely' Hungarian, Polish, German, French, or Christian.

Yet, the assertion of, search for, and preoccupation with, identity not just continues unabated, but keeps growing and invading ever more spheres of life. There are no indications that the identity wave is flattening. Not just psychologists emphasize that an identity is indispensable for a normal life. This is true in more than one sense. In the age of mass surveillance that takes shape equally in India's Aadhaar scheme, China's Social Credit System, and the databases of US secret services, every earthling has to be identifiable unambiguously and before long will be localizable with precision, night and day.

At the same time, identities in the material world dissolved into fluidity. Since Einstein taught us that there is no such thing as matter, objects have become 'space-time paths'. Common sense tells us exactly what an object is, but unity and identity of an object is not the same for theoretical physics and in everyday life.

The paradox of identity, then, is that it is not what it professes to be, true to itself. Or perhaps it is, like a chameleon, displaying different colours at different times, depending on the environment. Time is crucial. The duration of our stay on this earth is not very long. Since Socrates, this has changed only marginally. Although all those who dream of and support the preservation, 'forever', of various identities refer to the dim and distant past, the real measure of their projections may not extend beyond their lifetime.

Over the past half century or so, there has been a shift in our understanding from essence to construction and from discreteness to fuzziness of the identity of such things as race, religion, language, ethnicity, kinship, tradition, and even sex and life, while the methods and tools of individual identification have become more and more accurate. Is this a contradiction? If so, do we still know what we are talking about when talking about identity? Is there anything that deserves to be called a theory of identity that we can identify without stumbling from one battlefield of disputation to another?

In socially relevant domains, identities are borders, borders that separate independent countries, distinct ethnic groups and races, languages and their speakers, genders and sexualities, exclusive clubs, self-governing companies, and autonomous individuals. These units erect and defend their borders jealously. However, fixed as we may imagine them being, these borders are fluid and shifting. This is what identity apostles most fear; and it is hardly coincidental that the obsession with identity has reached new highs at a time when, in the Western world, migration across national borders is widely perceived as a threat.

Identity in whatever sense means sameness, but if we leave it at that, we are running in circles. Although Socrates saw many things, and although Leibniz's idea of the indiscernibility of identicals was and still is the clearest and most coherent definition of identity ever proposed, we have to recognize that the importance of identity then and now is different. This being so, identity today is, above all, our crown witness of a changing worldview imparted to us by scientific insights, technological innovation, and consumer capitalism—for better or worse.

Aspects of identity that are relevant to our present understanding include the following. First, the social and psychological concerns with identity are a product of modernity. This implies, next, that the concept is anchored in Western thinking. There therefore has to be an admission of the changeability of identity, both of any particular identity and of the concept. As part of modernization and Westernization, it spread around the world, prompting reflection about what is in the object and what is in our disposition to categorize the world around us. In the West, admonitions to avoid essentialism are of relatively recent origin, and with regard to identity not always heeded. By contrast, it has long been a guiding principle of Buddhist thought that identity is in the mind and not in the world. In keeping with such non-essentialist views, identity has moved from absolute sameness to perceived similarity, common interest, shared gods, shared space, shared history, and shared lifestyle. Further, because of the individualism that is part of modernization, the said attachments are no longer automatically and thus largely unconsciously acquired, but have become emotionally charged. The highlighted and sentimental character attributed to identity has increased its conflict potential. Without one you are nothing, while any particular feature of the multifaceted structure that is your identity both allows you to associate with others and exposes you to the dangers of exclusion and discrimination.

Individual identities are complex structures combining inherited features with various group memberships, loyalties, values, belief systems, and fashions. These structures adjust to changing circumstances and so does the concept of identity itself. Elements may be discarded or remixed, new ones added on occasion. Hence a definitive definition is not available. Instead, as an antidote to too much rigidity, we can refer to how the Samo of Burkina Faso understand identity, as cited by Italian writer Italo Calvino. It comprises nine elements:

(1) the body, which one receives from one's mother, (2) the blood, which one receives from one's father, (3) the shadow the body projects, (4) warmth and sweat, (5) breath, (6) life, or rather a particle of life, which is an entity in which all living beings are immersed, (7) thought, subdivided in understanding and consciousness, (8) the double, which is the immortal part that can perform and suffer witchcraft (it detaches from the body every night to wander in dreams, and then definitively some years before death to go on the journey of the dead where it will have two more lives and two more deaths of death, and finally it will incarnate a tree), (9) individual destiny.

References and further reading

References are listed in alphabetical order by chapter. They include all works cited and referred to as well as suggestions for further reading. Each chapter section ends with one or two relevant scientific journals.

Introduction: an 'identity' wave

Appiah, Kwame Anthony. 2018. *Mistaken Identities*. London: Profile.
Gapper, John. 2017. 'Goldman Sachs Suffers an Identity Crisis'. *Financial Times*, 17 October.
Gleason, Philip. 1983. 'Identifying Identity: A Semantic History'. *Journal of American History* 6: 910–31.
Hirsch, Eli. 1982. *The Concept of Identity*. Oxford: Oxford University Press.
Mackenzie, W. J. M. 1978. *Political Identity*. Manchester: Manchester University Press.

Chapter 1: 'Who am I?' Identity in philosophy

Descartes, René. 1641. *Meditationes de prima philosophia* [*The Philosophical Writings Of Descartes*, 3 vols, translated by John Cottingham, Robert Stoothoff, and Dugald Murdoch. Cambridge: Cambridge University Press, 1988].
Garrett, B. 1998. *Personal Identity and Self-Consciousness*. London: Routledge.
Grice, H. Paul. 1941. 'Personal Identity'. *Mind* 50: 330–50 <http://moglen.law.columbia.edu/twiki/pub/LawContempSoc/KalliopeKefallinosFirstPaper/Grice.pdf>.

Locke, John. 1689. *An Essay Concerning Human Understanding*, II, XXVII §11. London: C. and J. Rivington; T. Egerton and J. Cuthell <http://oll.libertyfund.org/titles/locke-the-works-vol-2-an-essay-concerning-human-understanding-part-2-and-other-writings>.

Montaigne, Michel de. 1580. *Essays of Montaigne*, book III, chapter 2. ed. William Carew Hazlitt, Volume 3. London: Reeves and Turner <http://onlinebooks.library.upenn.edu/webbin/gutbook/lookup?num=3600>.

Popper, Karl R. and John C. Eccles. 1977. *The Self and Its Brain: An Argument for Interactionism*. Berlin, Heidelberg, and New York: Springer.

Shoemaker, Sidney. 2003. *Identity, Cause and Mind*, expanded edition. Oxford: Oxford University Press.

Yao, Xinzhong. 1996. 'Self-construction and Identity: The Confucian Self in Relation to Some Western Perceptions'. *Asian Philosophy* 6(3): 179–95.

Philosophy <https://www.cambridge.org/core/journals/philosophy/>.

Chapter 2: Identity in logic and the classical law of thought

Frege, Gottlob. 1892. 'Über Sinn und Bedeutung'. *Zeitschrift für Philosophie und philosophische Kritik* 100: 25–50. 'On Sense and Reference', in Max Black and P. T. Geach (eds), *Translations from the Philosophical Writings of Gottlob Frege*. Oxford: Blackwell, 1952, 42–55.

Hájek, Petr. 2002. 'Fuzzy Logic', in Edward N. Zalta (ed.), *The Stanford Encyclopedia of Philosophy* <http://plato.stanford.edu/archives/fall2002/entries/logic-fuzzy/#1>.

Leibniz, Gottfried Wilhelm von. 1686. *Discours de métaphysique* [*Discourse on Metaphysics*] <http://www.earlymoderntexts.com/assets/pdfs/leibniz1686d.pdf>.

Morreau, Michael. 2002. 'What Vague Objects Are Like'. *The Journal of Philosophy* 99(7): 333–61.

Quine, Willard van Orman. 1960. *Word and Object*. Cambridge, MA: MIT Press.

Russell, Bertrand. 1971a [1908]. 'Mathematical Logic As Based on the Theory of Types', in R. C. Marsh (ed.), *Bertrand Russell: Logic and Knowledge*. New York: Capricorn Books, 59–102.

Russell, Bertrand. 1971b [1918]. 'The Philosophy of Logical Atomism', reprinted in R. C. Marsh (ed.), *Logic and Knowledge*. New York: Capricorn Books, 177–281.

Russell, Bertrand. 1997 [1923]. 'Vagueness', in Rosanna Keefe and Peter Smith (eds), *Vagueness: A Reader*. Cambridge, MA: MIT Press, 61–8.

Williamson, Timothy. 1990. *Identity and Discrimination*. Oxford: Basil Blackwell.

Wittgenstein, Ludwig. 1922. *Tractatus Logico-Philosophicus*. London: Kegan Paul, Trench, Trubner & Co.: 31.

Wreen, Michael. 2015. 'The Identity of Indiscernibles'. *Philosophy* 90: 33–57.

Logic Journal of IGPL <https://academic.oup.com/jigpal/>.

Chapter 3: Given or constructed? Identity in cultural anthropology

'"I Became a Black Man When I Arrived in England": Inua Ellams on His Play Barber Shop Chronicles'. *The Guardian*, 12 December 2017 <https://www.theguardian.com/stage/video/2017/dec/12/i-became-a-black-man-when-i-arrived-in-england-inua-ellams-on-his-play-barber-shop-chronicles>.

Barth, Frederik (ed.) 1969. *Ethnic Groups and Boundaries: The Social Organisation of Cultural Difference*. Boston and Oslo: Universitetsforlaget.

Dimitrovova, Bohdana. 2001. 'Bosniak or Muslim? Dilemma of One Nation with Two Names'. *Southeast European Politics* 2(2): 94–108.

Ethnic Group Statistics: A Guide for the Collection and Classification of Ethnicity Data. London: Office for National Statistics, 2003 <https://www.ons.gov.uk/peoplepopulationandcommunity/culturalidentity/ethnicity>.

Fish, Jefferson M. (ed.) 2002. *Race and Intelligence: Separating Science from Myth*. Mahwah, NJ: Lawrence Erlbaum.

Griffiths, Melanie. 2015. *Identity*. Oxford Bibliographies <http://www.oxfordbibliographies.com/view/document/obo-9780199766567/obo-9780199766567-0128.xml>.

Kakar, Sudhir. 1996. *The Colors of Violence: Cultural Identities, Religion, and Conflict*. Chicago and London: Chicago University Press.

Meissner, Fran and Steven Vertovec. 2015. 'Comparing Super-diversity'. *Ethnic and Racial Studies* 38: 541–55.

Purushotam, Nirmala S. 1998. *Negotiating Language, Constructing Race: Disciplining Difference in Singapore.* Berlin and New York: Mouton de Gruyter.

Roosens, Eugeen E. 1989. *Creating Ethnicity: The Process of Ethnogenesis.* Newbury Park: Sage.

United States Census Bureau. 2017. 'Race and Ethnicity'. <https://www.census.gov/mso/www/training/pdf/race-ethnicity-onepager.pdf>.

Weber, Max. 1922. *Wirtschaft und Gesellschaft: Grundriss der verstehenden Soziologie* [*Economy and Society: An Outline of Interpretative Sociology.* Berkeley: University of California Press, 1968].

Ethnicity, Identity and Migration Studies <http://www.fpce.up.pt/ciie/ciieinforma/2/4catalogue_Ethnicity_10.pdf>.

Chapter 4: Adam and Eve, Hijra, LGBTQs, and the shake-up of gender identities

Akerlof, George A. and Rachel E. Kranton. 2010. *Identity Economics: How Our Identities Shape Our Work, Wages, and Well-being.* Princeton: Princeton University Press.

Butler, Judith P. 1990. *Gender Trouble: Feminism and the Subversion of Identity.* New York: Routledge.

Dover, Kenneth James. 1989. *Greek Homosexuality.* Cambridge, MA: Harvard University Press.

Gibbon, Margaret. 1999. *Feminist Perspectives on Language.* London and New York: Longman.

Lips, Hilary M. 2008. *Sex and Gender: An Introduction.* Boston: McGraw-Hill.

Muehlenhard, Charlene L. and Zoe D. Peterson. 2011. 'Distinguishing Between Sex and Gender: History, Current Conceptualizations, and Implications'. *Sex Roles* 64: 791–803.

World Health Organization. *Gender and Genetics.* <http://www.who.int/genomics/gender/en/index1.html>.

Journal of Gender Studies <http://www.tandfonline.com/toc/cjgs20/current>.

Chapter 5: Identity in politics: promises and dangers

Anderson, Benedict. 1983. *Imagined Communities*. London and New York: Verso.

Elias, Norbert. 1991. *The Society of Individuals*. Oxford: Basil Blackwell: 208.

Engels, Friedrich. 1866. 'What Have the Working Class to Do with Poland?' *Commonwealth*, 24 March, 31 March, 5 May <https://www.marxists.org/archive/marx/works/1866/03/24.htm>.

Huntington, Samuel P. 1996. *The Clash of Civilizations and the Remaking of World Order*. New York: Simon & Schuster.

Keating, Michael. 2001. *Plurinational Democracy: Stateless Nations in a Post-sovereignty Era*. Oxford: Oxford University Press.

Mackenzie, W. J. M. 1978. *Political Identity*. New York: St. Martin's Press.

Moïsi, Dominique. 2009. *The Geopolitics of Emotion*. New York: Anchor Books.

Renan, Ernest. 1882. *Qu'est-ce qu'une nation?*, text of lecture delivered at the Sorbonne, 11 March 1882 <http://classiques.uqac.ca/classiques/renan_ernest/qu_est_ce_une_nation/renan_quest_ce_une_nation.pdf>; English translation: <http://ucparis.fr/files/9313/6549/9943/What_is_a_Nation.pdf>.

Rosanvallon, Pierre. 2011. *Democratic Legitimacy: Impartiality, Reflexivity, Proximity*. Princeton: Princeton University Press.

Sen, Amartya. 2006. *Identity and Violence: The Illusion of Destiny*. London: Penguin Books.

Weinstock, Daniel. 2006. 'Is Identity a Danger to Democracy?', in Igor Primoratz and Aleksandar Pavković (eds), *Identity and Political Self Determination*. Aldershot: Ashgate, 15–26.

National Identities: Critical Inquiry into Nationhood, Politics & Culture <http://www.tandfonline.com/toc/cnid20/current>.

Politics, Groups, and Identities <http://www.tandfonline.com/toc/rpgi20/current>.

Chapter 6: 'Your station in life': social identities in our time

Adorno, Theodor W. 1966. *Negative Dialektik*. Frankfurt: Suhrkamp [*Negative Dialectics*. Translated by E. B. Ashton. New York: Continuum, 1973].

Barthes, Roland. 2006. *The Language of Fashion*. London: Bloomsbury Academic.

Bauman, Zygmunt. 2004. *Identity: Conversations with Benedetto Vecchi*. Cambridge: Polity Press.

Bourdieu, Pierre. 1984. *Distinction*. Cambridge, MA: Harvard University Press [originally published as *La Distinction: Critique sociale du jugement*. Paris: Éditions de Minuit, 1979].

Brubaker, Rogers. 2005. *Ethnicity Without Groups*. Cambridge, MA: Harvard University Press.

The Chic Fashionista, 'Fashion Style Quiz' <http://www.thechicfashionista.com/fashion-style-quiz.html>.

Economic and Social Research Council. 2018. *Affluent Workers and Class Identity* <http://www.esrc.ac.uk/about-us/50-years-of-esrc/50-achievements/affluent-workers-and-class-identity/>.

Goffman, Erving. 1963. *Stigma: Notes on the Management of Spoiled Identity*. New York: Simon & Schuster.

Jenkins, Richard. 1996. *Social Identity*. London: Routledge.

Wacquant, Löic. 2008. *Urban Outcasts: A Comparative Sociology of Advanced Marginality*. Cambridge: Polity Press.

Social Identities: Journal for the Study of Race, Nation and Culture <http://www.tandfonline.com/loi/csid20>.

Chapter 7: Citizenship, legal status, and proof of identity: identity as a legal concept

Foster, Charles and Jonathan Herring. 2017. *Identity, Personhood and the Law*. Springer Briefs in Law, DOI 10.1007/978-3-319–53459-6.

Greenwald, Glenn. 2014. *No Place to Hide*. Toronto: Random House of Canada.

Mayer-Schönberger, Viktor and Kenneth Cukier. 2013. *Big Data: A Revolution That Will Transform How We Live, Work, and Think*. London: John Murray.

Murray, Elizabeth A. 2012. *Forensic Identification: Putting a Name and a Face on Death*. Minneapolis, MN: Twenty First Century Books.

Radden, Jenifer. 1996. *Divided Minds and Successive Selves: Ethical Issues in Disorders of Identity and Personality*. Cambridge, MA: MIT Press.

Saks, Michael J. and Jonathan J. Koehler. 2005. 'The Coming Paradigm Shift of Forensic Identification Science'. *Science*, 309: 892–5.

Shachar, Ayelet. 2009. *The Birthright Lottery: Citizenship and Global Inequality*. Cambridge, MA: Harvard University Press.

Weisman, Steve. 2014. *Identity Theft Alert*. Upper Saddle River, NJ: FT Press.

UN Convention on the Rights of the Child <https://www.unicef.org/crc/>.
Journal of Aging and Identity <https://link.springer.com/journal/10859>.
Journal of Forensic Identification <https://www.theiai.org/jfi/jfi_titles.php>.

Chapter 8: Selfhood and personality: the psychology of identity

Erikson, Erik H. 1956. 'The Problem of Ego Identity'. *Journal of the American Psychoanalytic Association* 4(1): 56–121.

Erikson, Eric H. 1970. 'Autobiographic Notes on Identity Crisis'. *Daedalus* 99: 730–59.

Freud, Sigmund. 1923. *Das Ich Und das Es*. Leipzig, Vienna, and Zurich: Internationaler Psycho-analytischer Verlag [*The Ego and the Id*. London: Hogarth Press and Institute of Psycho-Analysis, 1927].

Giddens, Anthony. 1991. *Modernity and Self-identity*. Stanford, CA: Stanford University Press.

Goffman, Erving. 1959. *The Presentation of Self in Everyday Life*. Garden City, NY: Doubleday.

Huskinson, Lucy and Murray Stein (eds) 2015. *Analytic Psychology in a Changing World: The Search for Self, Identity and Community*. London and New York: Routledge.

Riesman, David, Nathan Glazer, and Reuel Denney. 1950. *The Lonely Crowd: A Study of the Changing American Character*. New Haven, CT: Yale University Press.

Self and Identity: The Journal of the International Society of Self and Identity <http://www.tandfonline.com/toc/psai20/current>.

Chapter 9: 'They don't speak our language': identity in linguistics

Coupland, Nikolas. 2007. *Style, Variation and Identity*. Cambridge: Cambridge University Press.

Gibbons, John. 2003. *Forensic Linguistics*. Oxford: Blackwell.

Joseph, John E. 2004. *Language and Identity: National, Ethnic, Religious*. Basingstoke: Palgrave Macmillan.

Le Page, Robert and Andrée Tabouret-Keller. 1985. *Acts of Identity: Creole-based Approaches to Language and Ethnicity*. Cambridge: Cambridge University Press.

Llamas, Carmen and Dominic Watt (eds) 2010. *Language and Identities*. Edinburgh: Edinburgh University Press.

Molinelli, Piera (ed.) 2017. *Language and Identity in Multilingual Mediterranean Settings*. Berlin: DeGruyter Mouton.

Norton, Bonny. 2010. 'Language and Identity', in Nancy Hornberger and S. McKay (eds.), *Sociolinguistics and Language Education*. Clevedon: Multilingual Matters, 349–69.

Rickford, John Russell and Russell John Rickford. 2000. *Spoken Soul: The Story of Black English*. New York: Wiley.

Singh, Rajendra (ed.) 1998. *The Native Speaker: Multilingual Perspectives*. New Delhi and London: Sage Publications.

Thomas, George. 1991. *Linguistic Purism*. London: Longman.

International Journal of the Sociology of Language <https://www.degruyter.com/view/j/ijsl>.

Journal of Language, Identity, and Education <http://www.tandfonline.com/toc/hlie20/current>.

Chapter 10: Who is behind the mask? Identity in literature

Borges, Jorge Luis. 1964. 'Borges and I', in *Labyrinths: Selected Stories and Other Writings*, 246–7. New York: New Directions.

Dennis, Nigel. 1955. *Cards of Identity*. Harmondsworth: Penguin.

Gide, André. 1971. *Pretexts: Reflections on Literature and Morality*, translated by Justin O'Brien. Freeport, NY: Books for Libraries Press.

Hall, Peter. 2010. *Exposed by the Mask*. London: Oberon.

Jeffries, Lesley. 2017. *Stylistics*. Oxford Bibliographies <http://www.oxfordbibliographies.com/view/document/obo-9780190221911/obo-9780190221911-0048.xml>.

Jonsson, Stefan. 2000. *Subject Without Nation: Robert Musil and the History of Modern Identity*. Durham, NC: Duke University Press.

Pirandello, Luigi. 1922. *Six Characters in Search of an Author*, translated by Edward Storer. New York: E. P. Dutton.

Russell, Bertrand. 1905. 'On Denoting'. *Mind, New Series*, 14(56): 479–93.

Tuzzi, Arjuna and Michele A. Cortelazzo. 2018. 'What is Elena Ferrante? a Comparative Analysis of a Secretive Bestselling Italian Writer'. *Digital Scholarship in the Humanities* <https://academic.oup.com/dsh/advance-article/doi/10.1093/llc/fqx066/4818094>.

Double Dialogues <http://www.doubledialogues.com/>.

Conclusion: the identity of identity

Calvino, Italo. 1977. 'Identità'. *Civiltà delle macchine*, 25(5–6): 43–4.
Identity: An International Journal of Theory and Research <https://www.tandfonline.com/toc/hidn20/current>.

Publisher's acknowledgements

We are grateful for permission to include the following copyright material in this book.

Extract from Dimitrovova, Bohdana. 2001. 'Bosniak or Muslim? Dilemma of One Nation with Two Names'. *Southeast European Politics* 2: 94–108. By permission of Bohdana Dimitrovova.

Excerpt(s) from *Faust* by Johann Wolfgang Von Goethe, translation copyright © 1985 by Peter Salm. Used by permission of Bantam Books, an imprint of Random House, a division of Penguin Random House LLC. All rights reserved.

The publisher and author have made every effort to trace and contact all copyright holders before publication. If notified, the publisher will be pleased to rectify any errors or omissions at the earliest opportunity.

Index

SOCIAL MEDIA
Very Short Introduction

Join our community
www.oup.com/vsi

- Join us online at the official Very Short Introductions
  Facebook page.
- Access the thoughts and musings of our authors with our
  online **blog**.
- Sign up for our monthly **e-newsletter** to receive information
  on all new titles publishing that month.
- Browse the full range of Very Short Introductions online.
- Read **extracts** from the Introductions for free.
- If you are a teacher or lecturer you can order inspection
  copies quickly and simply via our website.

MEMORY
A Very Short Introduction
Michael J. Benton

Why do we remember events from our childhood as if they happened yesterday, but not what we did last week? Why does our memory seem to work well sometimes and not others? What happens when it goes wrong? Can memory be improved or manipulated, by psychological techniques or even 'brain implants'? How does memory grow and change as we age? And what of so-called 'recovered' memories? This book brings together the latest research in neuroscience and psychology, and weaves in case-studies, anecdotes, and even literature and philosophy, to address these and many other important questions about the science of memory - how it works, and why we can't live without it.

ADVERTISING
A Very Short Introduction
Winston Fletcher

The book contains a short history of advertising and an explanation of how the industry works, and how each of the parties (the advertisers , the media and the agencies) are involved. It considers the extensive spectrum of advertisers and their individual needs. It also looks at the financial side of advertising and asks how advertisers know if they have been successful, or whether the money they have spent has in fact been wasted. Fletcher concludes with a discussion about the controversial and unacceptable areas of advertising such as advertising products to children and advertising products such as cigarettes and alcohol. He also discusses the benefits of advertising and what the future may hold for the industry.

www.oup.com/vsi

DRUIDS
A Very Short Introduction
Barry Cunliffe

The Druids first came into focus in Western Europe - Gaul, Britain, and Ireland - in the second century BC. They are a popular subject; they have been known and discussed for over 2,000 years and few figures flit so elusively through history. They are enigmatic and puzzling, partly because of the lack of knowledge about them has resulted in a wide spectrum of interpretations. Barry Cunliffe takes the reader through the evidence relating to the Druids, trying to decide what can be said and what can't be said about them. He examines why the nature of the druid caste changed quite dramatically over time, and how successive generations have interpreted the phenomenon in very different ways.

www.oup.com/vsi

GLOBALIZATION
A Very Short Introduction
Manfred Steger

'Globalization' has become one of the defining buzzwords of our time - a term that describes a variety of accelerating economic, political, cultural, ideological, and environmental processes that are rapidly altering our experience of the world. It is by its nature a dynamic topic - and this *Very Short Introduction* has been fully updated for 2009, to include developments in global politics, the impact of terrorism, and environmental issues. Presenting globalization in accessible language as a multifaceted process encompassing global, regional, and local aspects of social life, Manfred B. Steger looks at its causes and effects, examines whether it is a new phenomenon, and explores the question of whether, ultimately, globalization is a good or a bad thing.